Discovering Your Core Values:

The Intentional Process of Discovering & Developing Biblical Core Values

By

Grady W. Strop & Richard A. Dungan

Cover Design by: Donna Macchi
ISBN 978-0-69-292107-4

Printed in the United State of America
First Edition

Rejoice Ministries International
www.rejoiceministriesinternational.com

DEDICATION

We dedicate this effort to our life partners, Sandy and Mary, who have helped us discover and establish life-giving core values. Also to the many men and women who have been mentors and examples of God-centered, biblically sound core values.

TABLE OF CONTENTS

FORWARD

As an avid outdoors person, I love to hike and bike. When venturing into an area that is unknown to me, I gather maps and trail guides, and engage with fellow adventurers who have previously traveled the route. The wisdom, insight, and encouragement received in this way have benefitted my journeys in countless ways. I have been able to embark upon the adventures with an increased sense of confidence, anticipation, and success.

This book is akin to a travel guide for life. In it, Grady and Dick have skillfully crafted a blend of biblical teaching, personal stories, and transparency, with a clear, practical path to guide you on the journey of establishing biblical core values in your life. These values will profoundly guide and influence all of your life decisions and relationships. As you follow the process given here, you can quickly get a bearing on where you currently are in regard to established core values and also gain clarity and understanding in additional steps to take to successfully navigate the life adventure awaiting you.

Regardless of your current life season, there is no better time to get wisdom and gain understanding of your core values than now. So, with this book, you can begin your journey to discover and further develop your core values in order to fulfill your destiny. As you take the steps in this process, I am confident the Lord will illuminate your life path toward your desired destination and you will finish well by His grace.

May your life journey be a profound adventure in Him.

Gary Yordy
Family Life Pastor
Living Faith Fellowship, Elkhart, Indiana

ACKNOWLEDGEMENTS

We both want to acknowledge a few people who have specifically offered help and encouragement toward seeing this book become a reality. Rarely does anything of value come without the input and work of many.

We want to thank the Rejoice Ministries Board of Directors and especially our chairman, David Schoening, for their consistent encouragement and challenge to put into book form what we have been teaching for many years. Without this, we would not have started or finished this project.

We would also like to thank our friend, Pastor Gary Yordy, who persistently and constantly encouraged and prodded us onward in starting and completing this effort. He was kind in his assessment of the value this book could have in the lives of those who might read and implement the concepts within it.

We want to express our thanks to Deb Wolff for her help getting us ready for publishing and with many other tedious details. We are also grateful for Donna Macchi for the cover art work.

We are so grateful and must acknowledge Kathy Borsa who definitely made this book readable. Her many hours of editing, comments, and suggestions have been immensely valuable to the final outcome. We are grateful for her patience with both of us as we entered the book writing process for the first time.

We thank the men and women who have engaged in the process of developing core values. We hope your efforts in engaging in the ideas and processes we have shared have been of value to all of you. Thank you for trusting us enough to take the chance of entering into and developing your core values.

Furthermore, we want to acknowledge the friends and loved ones in our lives who have exemplified life-giving values and have impacted our journey as we developed our values. They are too numerous to name, but God knows and we know how significant they have been in our lives.

Finally, we thank our wives and families. No one has impacted us more positively than our partners in life. Sandy and Mary, we love and thank you. Also, we thank our children who endured all the years of our journey toward seeking a life in Christ. They saw our true selves that were still developing and maturing. Thank you for all your patience, forgiveness, and the love you have shown us over the years of living together.

Grady & Richard (Dick)

INTRODUCTION

This endeavor began simply out of living life. Long before we had any terminology or idea of process, we found
ourselves in different situations of crisis and transitions
that forced us to delve into our own minds and hearts.
We had to figure out what we believed, why, and if it was
right. The Lord showed both of us grace as we sought to
figure out how to experience everyday life as followers of
Christ.

Through this journey, the Lord led us to a moment
of discovery. At the Denver airport, we both shared our
hearts regarding some significant values we had established accidentally or in times of crisis that had guided our
decisions to that moment. In the midst of that unplanned,
spontaneous discussion, we discovered a parallel experience that enabled us to begin to understand the significant power and positive impact of having clearly established core values in our lives. It was the beginning of a
new adventure, and now, this simple book.

From that day forward, we began to create a vocabulary, and eventually, a simple process to help us and others discover, evaluate, and create core beliefs and values
that guide our everyday decisions and choices. It really
has been an evolution of thinking and action that came

out of trying to live a life of following Christ. In our journey of life, we discovered this wonderful tool that has helped us both build a better life in Christ and experience deeper life-giving relationships. Our desire is to help others do the same. Over the past decade, we have incorporated this topic and process into the many ministry opportunities we have been a part of around the world. Retreats, conferences, small groups, and one-on-one discussions have been the opportunities we have used to share this tool with others to help them have a way to discover, evaluate, and then create biblical core values that can help them find victory in their everyday lives that face crisis, transitions, temptations, and ministry. This book is another attempt to help others discover and incorporate a way to be intentional about exploring the beliefs and values that lie deep in their minds and hearts.

We have intentionally tried to make it as short and concise as possible. We want men to read it! We also don't want to make something that should be easy and simple become complex or too overwhelming. It isn't rocket science. It is something that must come out of our personal journey with a real Savior and Lord. Our desire is to simply encourage and help the reader become aware of something that has always been a part of their lives. However, most haven't been consciously aware of the core values that already exist and control so much of their everyday lives.

It has been a difficult endeavor. There is so much more we wanted to share with the reader; however, we believed that being more concise and focused would be best. Yet, we still feel that what we have written is incomplete. So, we simply must trust one of our basic core values, "we know that the Holy Spirit and God's Word does the real ministry." We can only put our trust in what the Word of

God makes clear about His ability to speak to every mind and heart that chooses to seek Him. May He lead you into a personal, intentional journey of discovering and creating specific and foundational core values in your life.

Grady & Dick

SECTION ONE

Our Journey Toward Core Values:
How it Started

CHAPTER ONE

GRADY AND SANDY'S STORY

Sandy and I sat across from each other in one of the best restaurants in town. The original purpose and reason for the dinner escapes me, but I do remember that this mealtime was one of the most important events in our marriage, ministry, and future lives. Our conversation that evening was significant—becoming for me personally the most major relationship- and life-changing moment in our nine years of marriage.

My news that night was totally unexpected by Sandy, and she had some news for me too. Her announcement that we were going to have our fourth child was also unexpected, but nevertheless, good news!

What I had to say was not so good. Finding no easy way to unveil my news, I just blurted it out, "The elders of the church have asked me to take on the interim senior pastor position with an intention of making it a permanent position."

"Why?" she responded.

"Well, it's not good."

We had moved to this city and church six years earlier to join the staff of a small, struggling congregation. The senior pastor had arrived a few months previously and had invited us to come and join him and his wife in rebuilding

> *What guarantee did I have that I wouldn't fail?*

this broken church. Since he had been my best and closest friend since I was five years old, I had jumped at the opportunity to serve with him. Now, six years later, he was leaving for some unfortunate reasons.

I began to share what I currently knew of the story with Sandy. Life had been a whirlwind of overwhelming emotion and disbelief for the past few days. My best friend, pastor, and lifelong hero had failed big time. Now, his marriage, ministry, and successes were all in jeopardy, and everyone in his life would be affected. *My* life was in for a big change—that was for sure.

I won't share the nitty-gritty details, but the issue overwhelming me was: Am I healthy enough to take on this new role of senior pastor? The temptations that overtook my friend could as easily overtake me. I wondered if my marriage was strong and healthy enough to withstand the temptations that I knew could pass my way. What guarantee did I have that I wouldn't fail? Frankly, at that moment, I wasn't sure of the answers; I wasn't even sure I could go on. I actually suggested to Sandy that it might be time for me to quit the ministry and get as far from this situation as possible!

After much rambling, my focus began to change. If we did stay and I took the position of senior pastor, what could we do to protect ourselves from the same end result? That was the question that changed my life, my marriage, and my ministry forever. It was the beginning of creating intentional "core values."

I don't remember how long we sat there in the restaurant that night. We ate something, but I'm not sure what. Amazingly, I don't even remember paying the bill, even though I'm sure it was way out of our budget! The important thing that I *do* remember is that Sandy and I began a dialogue that would begin to establish intentional, specific, and healthy core values in our marriage and ministry. It would change our way of life from that day forward. That night and the whole experience that followed opened the door to the ministry we do now, more than twenty-seven years later.

My vocabulary didn't even include the term *core values* that night. In fact, even as I first began to share the concept with others, I didn't use that label. However, that was exactly what we were doing; we were creating intentional, specific core values for our marriage, relationships, and ministry. These were values that would clearly affect almost every decision and action we would take for the rest of our lives, and it has indeed been life-changing!

Now, fast forward sixteen years to the Denver airport where I was sitting with my good friend, Dick Dungan. We were on our way to lead a men's retreat in Texas. Dick and I had met in 1991 at a mission's conference in Omaha, Nebraska. From that time on, Dick was someone I could be real with, and he would always be real with me. He had become my spiritual coach. At this point, Dick had invited Sandy and me to join him on some short-term ministry opportunities in China with periodic trips over a couple of years.

I began to pour out my heart to Dick. After twenty-two years of pastoring in the same church, I had become somewhat complacent. Although it had been a great experience for my family and me serving at the church all these years, I had lost my enthusiasm and zeal for the day-to-day routine of pastoral ministry. The passion in my heart had shifted towards ministering to missionaries and church leaders.

As Dick and I sat in the airport, my heart was laid

before him. My passion for pastoring was gone, and I felt it might be time to make a change. I expressed to him that I was beginning to go against a few of the core values I had made with regard to my ministry. It was during this conversation that my talk of core values sparked something in Dick.

He began to share about some core values that he and his wife Mary had made many years before and how those values had guided them toward a healthier life in Christ. This talk about the idea of core values opened the door for a new adventure for both of us.

CHAPTER TWO

DICK AND MARY'S JOURNEY

For Mary and me, our journey into understanding the importance of biblical core values was quite different than Grady and Sandy's. We have discovered that, although each individual or couple's journey is unique to themselves, it is usually some type of crisis that causes a person to start asking the hard questions—questions like: "How did I get into this mess?" or "How do I avoid getting myself into *that* kind of trouble?"

The popular phrase "opposites attract" was certainly true in our case since our backgrounds were completely different. Mary was raised in a rural community farm family that worked from dawn till dusk pretty much every day. Her parents handled their finances in very conservative terms. Their spending was dictated by their income. For example, if they had a good harvest and prospered, then her father would upgrade his equipment; otherwise, he would find a way to make it through the next year with his existing equipment. They generally didn't borrow except for the purchase of the land they were farming. Although not considered wealthy in worldly terms, they certainly were viewed as financially stable and responsible people.

My life experience was quite different. My parents married very young; my father was eighteen and my mother not yet sixteen years old. My father was a hard worker, even holding down three different jobs at one time just to make ends meet for his rapidly growing family. But he had come from a very unstable family background. My grandfather was an alcoholic which eventually led to my father, the oldest of nine children, leaving home at the young age of fifteen. Although I certainly enjoyed and benefited from many good life experiences growing up, financial stability could not be considered one of them.

You can just imagine how these contrasting values clashed as, blindly in love, Mary and I launched into our marriage. By the grace of God, it has now miraculously been over fifty years, but it has not always been a smooth journey.

Sixteen years into our marriage and with three young children, we were in crisis—and I was the problem! I was guilty of just about everything a man could do to destroy his marriage, family, and life, but I will spare you the details. Suffice it to say, that although I had found a degree of success in sales and management in the corporate world, my lifestyle of drinking, gambling, and carousing, coupled with my poor financial decisions, had plunged us into a financial crisis!

> *We were in crisis—and I was the problem!*

Mary had been raised going to church every Sunday, and I had experienced going to Sunday school and church as a child and had even attended YFC (Youth for Christ) as a youth. But neither of us had entered into a personal relationship with Jesus Christ. That all changed in 1976 when a job promotion brought about our move to Kansas City. We had bought a place in the country, which was right across the road from a preacher—who obviously had something that I didn't have—a very real relationship with Jesus Christ!

It was in January of 1976 at a Sunday morning worship service that the Good News finally penetrated my heart that Jesus Christ had died for my sins, that He loved me, and that He would forgive me of *all* the ugly things that I had ever done. The realization washed over me that His precious blood which was shed on Calvary was shed for me and that He would cleanse me and make me whole. Wow! What a glorious day that was! That summer our twelve-year-old son Timothy asked Jesus into his life, and in November, Mary also gave her life to Christ.

In the next three years, there was miracle after miracle experienced both in my life and within our family. Through some very difficult but divine circumstances, we ended up returning to Mary's hometown of Norfolk, Nebraska. From the day I had come to Christ, the Holy Spirit began speaking to me in powerful, practical, and life-transforming ways through the Word of God. As I would read the Scriptures or listen to my pastor preach the Word, I found it speaking to me right where I was living—right in the crisis and reality of all my many poor financial decisions and past irresponsibilities. Yes, Jesus had saved me, but now the Holy Spirit was teaching me the process of sanctification and how to develop godly character.

The pressure of a substantial debt from a business failure, added to the weight of my previous financial irresponsibility, continually robbed me of hope for the future. During my devotional readings, I kept coming across Scriptures like: *"The rich rules over the poor, and the borrower is the slave of the lender"* (Prov. 22:7). Or: *"Owe no one anything, except to love each other, for the one who loves another has fulfilled the law"* (Rom. 13:8).

As I shared what I was experiencing with a brother who was discipling me, he immediately started asking probing questions about my personal finances. His assertive questions offended me somewhat at first, but it wasn't long before I realized the Holy Spirit was using him to speak truth in love. So great was my Heavenly Father's love for me that He was about to show me how to find freedom such as I had never known before.

My friend insisted that the next time we got together we would have a "credit card party"; we would cut up all our credit cards and establish a "cash budget envelope system." We would also attend a Christian financial planning seminar (*Christian Financial Concepts*, Larry Burkett). I was about to initiate the biblically-based core value that Mary and I have lived out for the past thirty-eight years. Desperate circumstances require extreme means, but the Word of God was revealing the values that we as His children were to live by.

We discovered such joy and sense of freedom in paying off each of those twenty-three creditors over the next eight years. In March of 1987, Mary wrote out the last check so that we could *"Owe no one anything, except to love."*

CHAPTER THREE

GRADY AND SANDY'S STORY CONTINUES

That evening at the restaurant, Sandy and I began to create specific and intentional core values in regard to our marriage and ministry. Of course, the term *core values* wasn't part of our vocabulary yet. We just realized we needed to make some clear constraints and standards based on biblical principles that would keep us (and in particular me) safe from falling into the same temptations to which so many others had fallen prey. Our first attempt was to make them practical, accountable, and maybe even measurable.

First, we started talking about our marriage. Up to this point in our marriage, we had been blessed with much grace. After nine years, we were still enjoying one another very much, and our marriage was good. We realized there had actually been a few core values made at the beginning of our marriage (though, of course, we had not fully understood what we were doing).

One of these values was that divorce would never be an option for us. This was a reaction to my family history in which divorce was very prevalent. From the beginning, we had determined that we wouldn't even mention the word—not even in jesting. As we talked about that decision, we actually realized how powerful it was and how it had given us the strength to avoid the divorce topic.

Maybe we were accidently on the right track!

However, the more we talked the more we realized that we had no plan in place to protect, strengthen, and cultivate our relationship together. Without consciously knowing it, a foundational core value had errantly crept in that said "Ministry is more important than -marriage," but, of course, I would never have admitted it. That had to change! Beginning that evening and over the next several months, I created and began to establish the internal core value that my marriage must come before my ministry. After that, we began to make several external or behavioral core values that would help this belief become true for both of us.

Therefore, our first step was to proclaim and establish clearly that our marriage was the most important human relationship we would have from this day forward. If our marriage was my most important ministry focus, then all other relationships, even within our church, would have to come second.

I was busy working part time at the church and working nearly full time at another job to make enough money for us to live on. Sandy was a stay-at-home mom, raising our three girls. Not only had she begun homeschooling the girls, but now we had another baby on the way.

As we talked, we discovered that we couldn't even remember the last time that we had taken a night out like this. It had been many, many months. Our first external *core value,* therefore, was to establish a date night once or twice a month.

Our relationship with our children would be next in importance; so that was our third core value. The church, my ministry, and the relationship to our congregation, colleagues, and others would have to come after these family relationships. I think these were the only three we established that evening in regard to our marriage. We didn't write them on paper at the time or make a certificate

> *Our first external core value: establish a date night once or twice a month.*

suitable for framing. We just spoke and agreed on these new values. However, for us, they were life changing and lifesavers.

Furthermore, I believe these clearly established values have allowed us to successfully continue in ministry all these years.

Next, we began to consider the ministry. What should we or could we do to protect ourselves (again, me particularly) from falling into a moral, ethical, or ministry-ending trap? Looking back now, I see that we had laid the foundational core value that Sandy and I wanted our calling and mission to do ministry to last for the long haul. We began to dialogue about the dangers and what we wanted to avoid. We discussed what actions we could take to guard against the possibility of even getting close to falling into the many snares Satan lays for all of those in ministry.

Over the next several weeks, I began to make our list of practical actions we would establish to create a safe and healthy environment that would help keep us on track. We consulted with Pastors and other sources to help us with this process. Some of the actions were:

- No one on our church staff (including me) would meet with the opposite sex privately outside of office hours or in isolated places.
- We would put windows in all office doors in the church. This would allow anyone the opportunity to look in at any time.
- Even with the above boundaries in place, I would not meet with a woman by myself more than one time. Sandy would be present for future meetings,

or I would delegate them to another woman for counseling or whatever was needed.

- I would take at least one day a week off to spend time with Sandy and the kids.
- I would take at least one two-week vacation each year.
- I would seek to have at least one "Paul" in my life, someone to provide a safe place where I could be real and accountable (Dick Dungan became the primary person for this action).
- We would protect our children from the negative aspects of church life and relationship issues by being careful not to speak in their presence about church issues that were difficult, unhealthy, unfair to us, or just plain ugly!
- We would protect our dinner hour (something Sandy always fought hard for). We would keep it consistent and make it a place of peace that would not be interrupted or lost to other things.

These are just some of the key actions that were put into place after we had established the core values of marriage, family, and ministry. Here you can see how core values overlap. Our foundational value to keep our marriage and family ahead of ministry connected to my ministry values.

That evening at the restaurant began our journey of establishing specific, intentional core values in our lives. We continued adding and building on specific core values and action points over the years leading up to the impromptu meeting Dick and I had at the Denver airport. Over a decade later, we are still adding to the list and seeking to help others develop their own journey with core values.

CHAPTER FOUR

DICK AND MARY'S CORE VALUES CONTINUED

The first foundational core value we established was: We will trust our God rather than the systems of this world to be the source of our provision.

We based it on Scripture promises:

And my God will supply every need of yours according to His riches in glory in Christ Jesus. (Phil. 4:19)

He who supplies seed to the sower and bread for food will supply and multiply your seed for sowing and increase the harvest of your righteousness. You will be enriched in every way to be generous in every way, which through us will produce thanksgiving to God. (2 Cor. 9:10-11)

For all the promises of God find their Yes in Him. That is why it is through Him that we utter our Amen to God for His glory. (2 Cor. 1:20)

Our second core value was: Mary and I will not allow any emotional walls to be established between our hearts!

As I mentioned earlier, after thirteen years of marriage without Christ, I had done just about everything a man could do to destroy his marriage. God was working in our lives to establish the first core value of *trusting Him to be our provision and helping us to live* free of debt while He was also working to heal the emotional pain in our lives and marriage.

Much of the pain that Mary and I contributed to each other's lives was rooted in the hurt that we had brought into our marriage due to our very different backgrounds. Beginning in May of 1980, the Holy Spirit began to reveal to me deep wounds that I would have to work through— bringing me to a point of forgiveness and exoneration for both of my parents.

As I worked through these areas of deep pain and received the Lord's healing presence, I began to see how inner vows that I had made had impacted the way I related to Mary and our children as well as others. This required that I take full responsibility for my words, attitudes, and actions by repenting before The Lord and seeking forgiveness from those I had hurt. Over the next four or five years, I began to learn the power of forgiveness and how to live in right relationship with the Lord and those I love. During this time, Psalm 15 and Psalm 24:3-5 became anchor Scriptures for my life.

"Who shall ascend the hill of the Lord? And who shall stand in His holy place? He who has clean hands and a pure heart, who does not lift up his soul to what is false and does not swear deceitfully. He will receive blessing from the Lord and righteousness from the God of his salvation." (Ps. 24:3-5)

The Holy Spirit convicted my heart countless times of sinful past issues—issues I needed to take responsibility for in order for relationships to be restored and healed. Learning to live with no "emotional bricks" between Mary's and my heart transformed the way we began to live our lives with one another and with others.

Little did I realize the significance of what God was doing in my life as He would quicken my spirit to powerful truths in these Scriptures. As I was learning the importance of not only reading the Word of God, but also memorizing and meditating upon these rich truths, the Holy Spirit was

> *He was putting His holy finger ... on the pain of my past.*

bringing revelation to me regarding the "hidden secrets'" of my past. Yes, I was certainly born again of the Spirit of God and forgiven, but in order for Mary and me to enjoy the oneness that He had sovereignly ordained for the covenant of marriage, He was revealing to me what it meant to walk in intimacy with Him. In the Lord's great love for me, He was putting His holy finger not only on the pain of my past, but also exposing the lies that I had believed and the deception that had bound me to the past.

During this time, I began to learn that the confession of my sin had to be as broad as the sin itself. If my sin was against God, then my confession was to be to God, but if my sin was against Mary (or others), then my confession had to be to her (or others) in order to have a clear conscience toward God and others.

One example that may seem a little extreme, but became a powerful learning and freeing experience for me, was taking responsibility for stealing a complete set of bath towels from the hotel that we stayed at during our honeymoon. My uncle had gifted us a two-night stay in the Honeymoon Suite at a very nice hotel from which I stole a beautiful set of bathroom towels. After I came to Christ and we had moved back to Nebraska in 1979, I would often drive by that hotel in Omaha. Although I had wonderful memories of our honeymoon, it wasn't those memories that kept coming back to me; it was the fact that I had stolen that set of towels.

I asked the Lord to help me understand why that kept coming up even though I knew that I had been forgiven. It was during this time that I came across Scripture about repaying "fourfold" what had been stolen (Ex. 22:1 and Eph. 4:28). After much wrestling, the Holy Spirit made it clear to me that I was to go back to that hotel, humble myself and pay them four times what those towels might have been worth. It seemed so crazy because almost twenty years had passed; the hotel wasn't even owned by the same company, and I would look like a fool! I did my research, priced an expensive set of bathroom towels, multiplied it by four and had Mary write out the check. I'll never forget the look on that young manager's face when I explained why I was there. He even tried to talk me out of it by telling me that it was all part of the cost of doing business. However, eventually he conceded to take my check once I shared my testimony of what Jesus Christ had done in my life and that it was more about my obedience to Christ and having a clear conscience than it was about the money!

God was using the past failures of my life to teach me about what it meant for me to become a man of godly character and integrity. As Mary watched me respond in obedience to God, she was growing in her ability to trust me.

Just the Beginning

This was the beginning of establishing clear and purposeful core values in our lives. The journey continues, and it has added to and safeguarded our lives in Christ and has made His truth more and more real in our marriages and ministries.

As you can see, our initial journey into discovering the need to establish life-changing core values came about from times of crisis and transition. It is in these situations, our core values, known and unknown, became revealed in our lives. However, we often, even in crisis, don't understand the significant influence and power our core values have in our choices and decisions!

Many times, the crisis is caused from an outside source or situation. However, often our unidentified core values, deeply hidden in our minds and hearts, are often the reason crisis overwhelms us or throws us into turmoil. In the past 30 years, we have made a discovery. If we are in an intentional and consistent process where we are identifying, carefully processing, and clearly creating biblical core values in how we do relationships and life, we don't have to let a crisis or transition control us with foolish reactions. We will be able to make healthy responses. These responses will lead us to growth and a deepening life in in Christ.

Even though neither the Dungan's or Strop's intentionally started to create core values, we found that life had brought us to a place of creating some clear points of belief, based on biblical grace and truth. In our conscious thinking, we could establish a determination to live out these beliefs in our everyday lives and relationships.

Over the years since that meeting at the Denver airport, we both (with our wives, colleagues, and many others) have continued to intentionally pursue the identity of the core values we already have in our lives and to rebuild those that are not based on biblical truth, emotional healthiness, and life-giving value. It has been an incredibly rewarding process and has given us much positive growth.

Our hope now is to help others to intentionally set a course toward identifying, establishing biblically-rooted values, and developing a greater ability to live out those values, bringing them into a life the Lord has for all those who live according to His life-giving grace and truth. We invite you to join us in this journey.

What Is a Core Value?

CHAPTER FIVE

DEFINING *CORE VALUE*

As we tried to more clearly define our experiences, we decided upon the term *core value*. Certainly, other terms suggest the same concept, also. Core principles, core philosophies, core beliefs, or core ideas could all be used interchangeably to describe what we call core values.

This is the term we have chosen to express the personal foundation upon which we have clearly established the principles we choose to live by. It is our goal to keep these principles biblical. Our decisions and actions flow from these intentional and specific values each and every day. These core values have allowed us to find a great deal of victory and health in our lives and in our relationships with others and with God.

We separate core values into two types: foundational/internal and behavioral/external. While these connect

> *It is within the foundational/internal core values where our faith and beliefs truly exist.*

with one another, they also have distinct elements. It is the foundational/internal core values we ultimately want to discover, explore and, if necessary, rebuild in our lives because they are truly what our behavioral values flow from. It is within the foundational/internal core values where our faith and beliefs truly exist.

In the end, our outward actions and behaviors will expose our foundational values. So, although we can identify, establish, and develop behavioral core value statements and actions, they will only be realized if we have the corresponding internal belief value in place. Therefore, as we define what a core value is, we are focusing upon the foundational/internal beliefs first and foremost. Primarily, the goal is not to just focus upon or change behavior (that is the goal of legalism). We want to experience a change of heart and mind toward a truer faith in Jesus Christ and His Word. We believe that is what brings life.

Grady: Let me give you a quick illustration of the separation. I was a tither since the age of 16. I gave 10% of my income to the church each month. This was an external behavior born out of a foundational core value or belief that God required me to establish this discipline. I had developed it based on the Bible's command to tithe. It was a responsibility and obligation that God did bless.

Fast forward 14 years when, at the age of 30, I had a revelation and recognized that my foundational core value was flawed. I discovered that what God's Word really taught (within the New Covenant) was that God wants me to believe that He is my provider and that I should tithe from this greater reality. Although my behavior of tithing didn't change, my reason for tithing changed completely. I started tithing because I believed God cared for me, and I could trust Him with all my financial needs. Therefore, I tithed out of faith in this reality and did it from a grateful heart, not out of responsibility and obligation. When this internal belief changed, I became a cheerful tither and even began to give above and beyond 10% of my income. So, when we speak of core values we are primarily focused on the foundational/internal beliefs in our hearts and minds.

What is a Foundational/Internal Core Value?

Foundational/internal core values are:

- The underlying beliefs and principles established in one's mind and heart. *"For as he thinks in his heart, so is he…" (Prov. 23:7 NKJV).*

- From the specific and foundational beliefs and principles that a person has in his mind and heart generates all their criteria and standards for decisions and actions in their lives.

Everyone *has* core values. However, most of us, even followers of Christ, have never really considered, explored, or intentionally established them. It's as if we live our lives on autopilot, without even knowing it! Every day, every moment, we are making decisions and acting upon a set of values we haven't even realized are there.

Often, we make intellectual, external/behavioral core values without discovering or understanding the corresponding internal/foundational core value in our hearts. Again, this connects to the "original" core value of self-love and pride. Just knowing commands and rules is never enough—we need to know what is at the core of God, His love, and nature. Only then can we come to know our true self because of His work that gives us the foundational core values that we need to live as He created us to live.

Under the Old Covenant, the Israelites tried to live by the Ten Commandments. They had the best list of external/behavioral core values ever written, but without faith in the foundational core values that God was first and foremost love and loved them, they only knew how to seek self-righteousness. They missed the two great core values and commands that He desired for them to believe: to *"love the Lord God with all your heart and with all your soul and with all your might"* (Deut. 6:5) and that God loved them so much that He had made them a people—His people. This reveals the difference between internal/foundational core values and external/behavioral core values.

If we merely seek to obey the external/behavioral commands and values, we will end up being only religious and legalistic. However, if we place our faith and trust in the reality of God at His core of love, we will experience a life-giving relationship with the Triune God, and His love will flow from our behavior into those around us—even the lost!

I didn't understand this distinguishing for many years. I became focused and intentional about discovering, recreating, and establishing external or behavioral core values. Often this process would lead me back to the foundational truth that I needed to recognize and establish my faith upon so that the external values connected to the real and personal God and not just His commands.

After that night at the restaurant, I began to establish core values in different areas of my life. I started with marriage and ministry, but I also began to see the value of getting more specific. What were my core values as a father to my children? I recall sitting one day at my desk at the church thinking about how so many pastors' children end up a mess in their relationship with God and the Church. So, I began to write a foundational/internal core value regarding my children. "I will do all I can to help my children love God and love the Church."

Then, I wrote down some strategies and external/behavioral guidelines to help make this value a valid reality:

- I won't force them to be at church every time the door is open.
- I won't place unrealistic or unfair expectations on them just because they are "the pastor's kids."

- If they are being affected negatively at the specific church we are at or because of my ministry, I will make a change.
- I will do my best to allow them to find their "niche" within the different ministries within church life.
- I will do my very best to attend their activities and be involved in their personal lives outside of church also.

This list was my starting point that day. Again, as the months and years passed, the list grew. It was often after making a mistake or discovering other issues or ways of thinking that I had to reevaluate and rework the behavioral guidelines I had in place in this area of my life. However, the foundational value to "help my children love God and love the church" didn't change.

For example, I realized the power of making promises that I couldn't or didn't keep. Even though my children are all adults now, they often remind me of a promise I apparently made one day to build them a tree house. I honestly don't remember making such a promise. I know I talked about it many times, but a *promise*? Whatever I said, it must have come out sounding like a promise to them. Perhaps I let the word *promise* slip out during one of those times I talked about a tree house.

One of my foundational core values as a father is to be "trustworthy like God is to me." Therefore, after that, I established a behavioral core value or guideline to not make promises to my children that couldn't be kept!

Our goal is to make our action or behavioral core values stem from the principle of our foundational belief and value that we hope is biblically revealed. They are not merely rules or action statements (even though they certainly affect actions). They are guidelines that are based upon a foundational principle. Therefore, promises that I can't keep to my children make me a liar, express to them that I don't value them, give them the wrong image of their heavenly Father, and don't display integrity. You get the picture. Every core value has to be built from and upon a principle and, for me, should also be biblically supported.

The additional reality to understand here is that we can make all the external/behavioral values we want, but if they are not connected to a real and solid biblical foundational/internal core value, we will fail in the application of our good intentions. In this case, my wanting to help my children love God and the Church would only be successfully realized if my actions came out of a true belief in my heart. As I look back on my attempt to implement these external values there was some failure because my belief in the core value wasn't always as established in my heart and mind as I had hoped. I had to keep growing and practicing my core belief. However, because I had identified it and clearly defined it, I did accomplish it in a greater way than if I had not established it and attempted to learn how to act upon it.

Therefore, a foundational core value is one that is formed from our relationship with God and His Word. It is a declaration of and a commitment to a specific truth that we place our faith in. In this way, grace and truth in our lives.

CHAPTER SIX

A BIBLICAL CASE FOR CORE VALUES

Human history begins with the establishment of a couple of significant commands that God wanted Adam and Eve to faithfully follow. These could be called external or behavioral values. However, there was a foundational core value or belief that these commands were based on, and it is important to see this distinction.

The Creator wanted a relationship with Adam and Eve. He wanted them to be loved and blessed by Him, and His desire was that they would return love to Him by their own choosing. It is from this foundational value that He gave them a couple of needed external/behavioral values, commands, and guidelines. These would help them live in the healthy, life-giving relationship with Him that He intended for them to experience.

The Creator gave the first value to apply to their new existence and lives when he gave the following command to Adam and Eve:

> Be fruitful and multiply and fill the earth and subdue it and have dominion over the fish of the sea and over the birds of the heavens and over every living thing that moves on the earth. (Gen. 1:28)

This command was based upon God's core value for humankind to "create," "rule over," and be stewards of the earth which was God's gift to them.

The second directive to be established in their heart and obeyed was:

But of the tree of the knowledge of good and evil you shall not eat, for in the day that you eat of it you shall surely die. (Gen. 2:17)

This command was given as a guideline or external value to help them stay true in their faith to God. It was necessary in order to experience and fulfill God's purpose for their lives that was born of the foundational core value He had given them. Their failure to abide by this core value proved to be their downfall.

Adam and Eve's ability to obey this command had to be based upon the core value of faith in God. To be successful in obeying this command required a value and belief in the reality of God's love for them. He had created an environment that provided them all they would ever need—even protection from death. Wanting them to love Him from a heart that is free, God then gave the requirement for devoted belief in Him.

One day, one of the "creeping things" which they had dominion over challenged this requirement and value for their faith and belief in God and His Word. The serpent offered them a different foundational core value to believe in that was in direct opposition to what God had spoken to them. He accused God of lying, suggesting they consider another possible reality and place their belief in his lie that proclaimed: "you will be like God" (Gen. 3:1-7). And you know the rest of the story!

They had exchanged their faith and belief from God and the promise of His love for them to a new core value. Now they would live by making their decisions and acting upon the belief that they could be their own god and get along just fine relying on self-love. This core value of self-love we call pride. When they began to live from this new core value, their world was changed in every way as it ushered in the consequence of the curse. From the beginning of humanity, we can see the reality and power of core values. We can also see that there are both good core values and bad core values.

We are fortunate that God's core value (who He is) is love. If He were not true to His core, we wouldn't stand a chance. His perfect love for us has been the life-giving reality of human history. Humankind is engaged in the continual battle between God's value of loving us (God's kingdom) and our continued belief in the lie of self-love and pride (man's kingdom).

This foundational core value issue is what establishes who we are (or believe we are) and our entire core values are birthed and established from it. We will look more closely at this foundational core value later. The Bible and all of history's record reveal humankind's story of this battle between these two primary core values or beliefs.

Scriptures reveal that humankind has struggled down through history to decide which of these is the truth. Do we place our basic life belief in God's Word of love for us or do we choose to make love for self (pride) our foundational core value? In other words, what foundational core value do we place our faith and trust in? We have two primary and foundational core values that all other core values emerge from: faith in God or faith in ourselves! History reflects that humanity tends to default toward the latter. Apart from God's original core value, we are left with the lesser value of human pride or self-love. When this happens, most of our other core values are established from this primary error of belief.

A multitude of examples of this ongoing struggle can

be found in the Bible. The following are examples of core value statements from the Word of God:

- Genesis 4:9: *". . . am I my brother's keeper?"* Cain felt that he was unfairly treated and abandoned by God, and then he determined that murder was an appropriate action.

- Joshua 24:15: *"As for me and my house, we will serve the Lord."* Joshua had gathered all of Israel together to make a decision and renewal of their covenant to God. After telling the story of God's perfect and continual love and blessing to them in verses 1-13, Joshua told them to *". . . choose this day whom you will serve . . ."* They had to establish a core value to either believe God or serve all the other false gods around them. But Joshua's core value was already established. He and his family would choose to serve God and believe fully in His love and care for them.

- Within the story of Job, he shares several core values that keep him from cursing God and losing the battle with his devastating, though temporary, afflictions.

- The entire book of Proverbs states external/behavioral core values of a wise king that offers a fulfilling life in the reality of God's foundational value of His truth and love.

- Daniel 1:8: *"But Daniel resolved that he would not defile himself with the king's food, or with the wine that he drank."* In the midst of an ungodly culture, Daniel chose as his core value that he would not succumb to the defiling ways around him. He trusted that God's care for him would allow him to rise above the circumstances of a most difficult life situation.

- Luke 4:18-19: *"The Spirit of the Lord is upon me, because He has anointed Me to proclaim good news to the poor. He has sent Me to proclaim liberty to the captives and recovering of sight to the blind, to set at liberty those who are oppressed, to proclaim the year of the Lord's favor."* Jesus understood from Scripture what His calling and purpose were, and He established it clearly in His heart and mind that He would follow God's Word for His earthly life and mission to display God's love for humankind.

- Philippians 1:21: The apostle Paul proclaims, *"For to me to live is Christ, and to die is gain."* Paul is able to stay in the battle of ministry because of this core value he has distinctly established. He would love to go home to the Lord but can, and will, stay in the battle of ministry for the *"progress and joy in the faith"* of those God has called him to serve.

These are just a sample of the core values cited in the Bible. With a little focused observation, one can see the foundational importance of establishing sound, God-centered and God-proclaimed core beliefs. It is not a side issue; it is a central and essential need. We each have to know what we believe and what (or who) we place our faith in every day of our lives.

In James 5:8, James challenges the reader to *"Establish your hearts, for the coming of the Lord is at hand."* I believe the process of establishing in one's heart true faith in Christ Jesus and all He has proclaimed is the intentional journey of discovering and establishing our core values. This is mandated in Scripture from beginning to end. It isn't a philosophy or ideology we've created; it is part of a disciple of Christ's calling to live out intentionally every day. To win the battle between pride and faith in Jesus

Christ is truly possible when we establish clear, biblical core values in our minds and hearts.

We must come to know

"... the knowledge of God's mystery, which is Christ, in whom are hidden all the treasures of wisdom and knowledge. I say this in order that no one may delude you with plausible arguments." (Col. 2:2-4)

This was Paul's deep desire for the Colossians. He wanted them to find God, place their full faith in His truth, and live in the fullness of His love for them. He wanted them to experience the victory of being a son or daughter and fulfilling their destiny.

Paul also states:

Therefore, as you received Christ Jesus the Lord, so walk in Him, rooted and built up in Him and established in the faith, just as you were taught, abounding in thanksgiving. (Col. 2:6-7)

Finding and establishing your core values in Christ is part of the process and journey of being rooted and built up in the faith. Paul also shares this need to be *"established"* in his other epistles or letters to the believers he serves.

In Ephesians 3:14-21, Paul prays and encourages his readers to be *"rooted and grounded" (vs. 17)* in the reality of God's comprehensive and boundless love! He is declaring a significant core value they need to establish in their minds and hearts. If they will believe and trust in God's overwhelming love for them, they will be *"filled with all the fullness of God"* (vs. 19).

In 2 Corinthians 10:3-6, Paul suggests that *"... arguments and every lofty opinion raised against the knowledge of God ..."* are wrong core values. We want to *"take every thought captive to obey Christ ..."*

Every Thought

In Him, the *true Word,* we discover and establish life-giving core values. An unhealthy core value is a value or belief that is contrary to God's truth. The process of creating biblical core values is the tearing down of strongholds (such as lies and wrong thinking) and establishing strongholds of truth and life. We are taking back the ground that so often has been given over to Satan's lies and giving it back to the Lord!

The Scriptures reveal that our foundational core value must be knowing and believing that God loved us since the moment we were created, and He wants us to have an intimate relationship with Him as a son or daughter. However, we are born under the wrong foundational core values of pride and self-love that cause us to be orphans*. Yet, when we confess that Jesus is Lord and believe in our hearts that God raised Him from the dead, we are saved (see Romans 10:9, 10).

At the point we surrender the core value of self-love (pride) to Jesus Christ, we truly are born again and begin a new life in Him, and it begins to change every aspect of our lives. From this greater core value, we can begin to build (or rebuild) all of our life relationships, decisions, and actions upon this truth. This is the journey we are on.

Discovering this relational reality, we can now begin to establish the external/behavioral core values and they bring us into—and keep us in—the better life our heavenly Father, Son, and Holy Spirit have always wanted us to know and experience. It leads us into a journey back to His original plan of living life as a son or daughter in daily relationship with Him.

* We recommend *No Longer Orphans* by James Macchi for an in-depth consideration of this significant life issue.

SECTION THREE:

Finding Your Core Values

CHAPTER SEVEN
YOU ALREADY HAVE THEM!

Establishing core values is definitely a spiritual journey that results in foundational spiritual formation. However, it is also a very tangible and practical process. There are some very simple steps one can take to build clear, life-giving core values.

There are some simple and practical steps you can implement on this life-giving journey. They will lead you toward building a structure that will help you develop life-giving core values. What we are offering is not theory but something real, workable, and applicable; something that establishes value in your life. First, we need to express some basic assumptions we believe to be true regarding core values.

Assumption #1:

Foundational core values are already established in everyone's mind and heart. Upon this foundation, our faith is grounded, and all our decisions and actions in life flow from it daily.

Assumption #2:

Most people have never given much thought to discovering or analyzing their core values and beliefs. They are unaware how their decisions and actions are determined or from where they originate.

Assumption #3:

Many Christians have created or established external behavioral core values without clearly identifying the foundational/internal core value of God's love for them. Without this core value being clearly discovered and established, they struggle to achieve joyful obedience to the external values they seek to live out. This leads to religion and legalism much like the Pharisees experienced.

Assumption #4:

The core values and beliefs that most people have are not established upon the Word of God. Therefore, their trust is based on deception

> *The core values and beliefs that most people have are not established upon the Word of God.*

instead of on God's truth. Because of this reality, most people (including Christians) are continually defeated in specific areas of their spiritual, mental, emotional, and relational existence. They are double-minded:

> *Count it all joy, my brothers, when you meet trials of various kinds, for you know that the testing of your faith produces steadfastness. And let steadfastness have its full effect, that you may be perfect and complete, lacking in nothing. If any of you lacks wisdom, let him ask God, who gives generously to all without reproach, and it will be given him. But let him ask in faith, with no doubting, for the one who doubts is like a wave of the sea that is driven and tossed by the wind. For that person must not suppose that he will receive anything from the Lord; he is a double-minded man, unstable in all his ways. (James 1:2-8)*

> *Submit yourselves therefore to God. Resist the devil, and he will flee from you. Draw near to God, and He will draw near to you. Cleanse your hands, you sinners, and purify your hearts, you double-minded. (James 4:7-8)*

Assumption #5:

As a Christian grows in the knowledge of God's truth and in relating to the Father, Son, and Holy Spirit, internal/foundational and external/behavioral core values can and should change. This is the journey of discipleship and Spiritual development.

Where Do Our Core Values Come From?

Grady: As I began to intentionally consider my core values, I slowly discovered where my underlying values had been conceived and established. I came to realize that I was born with a foundational core value of pride. After that significant realization, I began to identify other areas of my life that had contributed in establishing my core faith and values.

My family system was the next most significant influence. I think I can safely say that nearly all the core values formed in my first ten years of life came from my family. My early beliefs and faith (what I believed about myself, God, others, and life itself) were shaped within the small world and environment of my parents and family and their beliefs. This is typical as much of one's self is developed in these early years. However, many other factors outside of my family system influenced my life and beliefs as well. Some of these outside influences reinforced what I received from my family, but some of their input opposed what I had learned or picked up from my family system.

In my early teen years, these outside influences began to have a major impact on the establishment of my core beliefs. These outside influences often offered opposing ideas to those I had received and believed from my family system ushering conflict and confusion into my life. Some of these new influences initiated changes and adjustments in my core values. These were, somehow accidental in nature, and I'm not sure I was even aware of the change.

As I grew older and my world expanded, my core values were constantly challenged. I was learning to rethink some of the beliefs and values that I had held to in the past, specifically with the external things in my life. However, in the internal areas of my life, I held onto much of what I had believed from my childhood about myself, others, God, and the world around me. It would take many more years for me to even look deep inside myself to discover clearly who I was and who God was in my life—and exactly what all of that meant.

God created man with a few basic core values and belief requirements. We were created to have a loving relationship with our Creator. He didn't *impose* this belief upon Adam and Eve, but God apparently wanted humankind to freely choose whether to believe or not believe in the love of their Creator. He wanted them to choose to reciprocate this love. This is what makes us different from the rest of His creation.

In the incredible environment God had created, Adam and Eve could live in a loving relationship with Him, nature, and one another. They had the opportunity to trust in His love and provision for them every day. It truly was paradise. It went smoothly for a while, and they had it all.

There was an adversary, though, determined to steal away from Adam and Eve all that God had given them. His goal was to destroy their relationship with one another, and even more so, with God. Satan's plausible argument was an attempt to break down their trust, and therefore, the loving relationship between them and their Creator. Still active today, the same adversary continually tries to persuade us to live by a destructive core value of trusting in a foundational lie of self-love instead of God's love.

Adam and Eve were given one major boundary. Within

this boundary, God also gave them a choice to trust Him and place their faith in His word of truth. They could choose to obey His boundary and make it their core value. However, He had also left it possible for them to choose to do otherwise. Satan came presenting a lie that tempted them to trust in themselves. If they stepped across that boundary and tasted the forbidden fruit, they could be *"like God"* (Gen. 3:5). This challenged them to choose what to believe. Was God telling the truth or was He a liar? When presented the opportunity to believe something and someone other than God, they chose to establish a new core value—pride or self-love. This set humankind on a course that would establish self-love as their basic core value. This foundational core value that we are born with becomes the nucleus around which everything in the world revolves.

When people see the fallacy of this value, after salvation and through their growth in understanding who they now are in Christ Jesus, they can be redeemed from the foundational lie of pride. They can establish not only a new core value of faith in God's love for them but they can also rebuild all the other wrong values that control all the aspects of their lives. Experiencing complete conversion, they can grow to live once again as God created humankind to live—in right relationship with Him and one another.

Family Systems

Dick: As I reflect on my early years, I've come to realize that many of the values that I carried into my adult years and marriage were rooted in my life experiences from childhood and what we refer to as "family systems." Although there were certainly numerous good things for which I'm grateful, such as my work ethic passed down from both of my parents, there were also many unhealthy 'core values' that had a negative impact on Mary's and my relationship as well as our children and others we were around.

My life as a child seemed to always be on an emotional roller coaster with current circumstances dictating the atmosphere of our home. When things were going well, life was good, but when things were not going so well, there was conflict between my parents which usually meant that alcohol was involved—and fear filled the atmosphere.

There were times when our father was absent for longer intervals, and being the only boy, I became the man in the family. At one point in time, when I was thirteen, my father was working out of state, my mother had been in a car accident and was bedridden, my older sister was not living with us, and my three younger sisters were all looking to me for their care and protection. This was an emotionally difficult time for me as a young boy which resulted in my taking on responsibility that God didn't intend for a young boy to carry. This situation would later have a huge impact on how I related to my younger sisters. As we all grew into adulthood, got married, and started our own families, my sisters continued to come to me for advice and help which isn't bad in and of itself, but usually they would be pursuing me when they should have been taking their cares, concerns, and burdens to their own husbands. There were times when I couldn't figure out why my brothers-in-law didn't seem to want to relate to me. Eventually I discovered that they resented me because their wives (my sisters) were frequently comparing them to me.

Even after I became a Christian, I found that when one of my sisters would call me over the years for advice, counsel, or help, I would have this terrible feeling come up inside of me that wanted to tell them "leave me alone!" I would listen, but in my heart, I resented them bothering me. It was amazing that I could minister to people in

our church or total strangers with great freedom and insight from the Lord, but when it came to my own flesh
and blood, I hated it and felt resentment toward them.
Obviously, this was unhealthy for their marriages as well
as our relationships.

It would be several years before the Lord would help
me discover the source of the guilt and shame that taunt-
ed me because of the way I felt toward my own sisters
who had also become followers of Christ.

While attending a marriage conference in celebra-
tion of Mary's and my thirty-fifth anniversary, the time
was right for the Holy Spirit to bring light into this area
of darkness and deception. God had already brought so
much healing into our lives and marriage that we were
already mentoring couples and teaching on marriage.
However, during one of the "practical exercise" times, I
shared with Mary that the Holy Spirit had reminded me
of this unhealthy feeling I had toward my sisters, and she
suggested that we should ask the retreat facilitators for
insight and prayer.

As I shared my story, it was amazing how quickly the
facilitator brought insight into my situation. He shared
that when our family was in such turmoil during my early youth, I had become a surrogate father to my three
younger sisters. Although there was a need for me to help,
protect, and care for my sisters, it was not God's design or
intent for the unhealthy soul ties that came out of that experience. During prayer, the Holy Spirit revealed to me the
moment in my thirteen-year-old heart that I had decided
that "everything depended on me" and that I had to become "self-reliant" to care for my mother and sisters. It was
so liberating to renounce that lie and repent of my self-
sufficiency. The Holy Spirit led me to go to my sisters, one
at a time, asking their forgiveness for the rejection that my

responses to their situations caused in their hearts. Then I asked them to set me free from being the surrogate father, so that I might truly be the brother the Lord intended for me to be.

Grady: Family matters! We were predominantly a blue-collar family. My stepfather was a union man and a democrat, while my Uncle Wayne was a Barry Goldwater conservative republican. Their raucous political debates provided entertainment for our Thanksgiving meals. As a young boy, I listened to them debate their conflicting views, and then, during my teen years, I had to decide what would be my own personal core values when it came to politics. No matter which choice I made, it still came primarily from my family. But this was just one of many areas.

Early in life, much of who I was revolved around the core values of my family. As I grew into adulthood, I duplicated or reacted to my family's core beliefs. Family is powerful in the establishment of most of our core values. Most often, we live unaware of these deep-rooted values despite making all our daily life choices out of them. We need to reexamine these family values and see if they are true and compatible with God's Word and Spirit, realizing that we were created to live from His family core values.

One example from my life regarding the power of family as it relates to our core values of life and living can be seen in how the Strop family managed conflict! Right off, let's say we didn't do it well. I'm not sure we ever resolved many important issues within the four walls of our home. There was a lot of yelling, anger, and emotional hurt without much healing or growth.

Often, after a significant period of angry yelling, my stepfather would get in his car and leave the house for a few hours. Later, when he returned, we all coexisted silently for the rest of the day and evening. The next morning, we just went on living together as if nothing had happened. We all learned how to live in this way of dealing with conflict—it's called dysfunctional.

So, then I married Sandy, and we were enjoying life together. I was thrilled that I had a fresh start at how to do family. I was going to do everything better than my dad and mom did regarding marriage and family. Then we had our first significant conflict over something totally insignificant—honestly, I don't remember what the conflict was even about. I do remember an outburst of angry words (mostly from my mouth), and I left our apartment and headed to the car. I didn't drive anywhere; I remember sitting in the car, in a daze, wondering what had just happened and realizing that I was duplicating my parents' family system.

Sandy's parents had taught her, *"Be angry and do not sin; do not let the sun go down on your anger"* (Eph. 4:26). Over the next several years, with Sandy patiently encouraging me, I began to purpose in my heart to quit fleeing and start communicating—both talking and listening. Ultimately, I changed my core value from "flee from conflict" to "talk it through" with the goal to understand the one I am having the conflict with, starting the process the day of the conflict.

The conflict isn't always immediately resolved—that can take months. But we work through and remove any anger, getting ourselves to a safer emotional condition. At that point, we can begin to "speak the truth in love" which can lead us to healthy change and resolution.

When I realized that I needed to change my method of handling conflict, I could identify a healthier way and differentiate a new approach of engaging in and even resolving conflict. I must admit that, even now, after years of making this core value a part of my life, I can still default to the "flee" value. However, it has become much more natural for Sandy and me to quickly get through the initial emotional reaction and move into identifying the real issue as we talk and listen to each other. Then we can create a plan to make a change.

Once a person decides to delve into the process of discovering and rebuilding their core values, they will have to revisit their past and consider the family they grew up in. As I mentioned earlier, much of who we are and how we do life is established from our family of origin's core values. There are unhealthy and unbiblical values in most family systems, but those flawed values can change. It may take a few generations to get them all fixed, but more and more, we can live in the life-giving values God has for all those who have chosen to live in His family.

The Powerful Influence of Models and Mentors

Many years of being intentional in discovering my core values and reshaping and establishing healthy and biblical values in their place have made me realize the powerful influence that many people had in the development of my core values and beliefs. Beyond my family of origin, there have been a few others in my life who have had a major impact in that development.

I define *models* as those who had some significant influence in my life without necessarily having any deep relational connection. These include, but are not limited to, teachers, friends, peers, cultural figures, specific speakers or authors, and employers.

On the other hand, *Mentors* would be those who had influence in my life *with* a deep relational element. Therefore, their influence was much more powerful and had a greater impact on my core value development. These influencers came from the same arenas of life as models (for example, teachers and pastors) but were much more involved in my life. I trusted them, and in some cases, I had a strong desire to imitate them. Mentors have a very powerful place in our lives and can, at some point, even become more influential in our life development than our parents and family systems. For most individuals, this begins to take shape in late childhood.

For myself, a couple of pastors had the greatest impact in shaping my world view and core values. Often, their influence directly opposed the values I had learned from my family. This certainly created some relational conflict (inwardly and outwardly) with those in my nuclear family. However, these mentors offered a healthier alternative that was significantly valuable for me. Ultimately, it was because of these mentoring relationships that I chose to go into full-time ministry as a pastor. Talk about imitating!

Three Bobs Who Helped Shape My Life in Christ!

Dick: Over the years of my life, even before I came to Christ, God sovereignly brought many individuals into my life that influenced and impacted me greatly. Without realizing it, God was building into my life core values based on biblical truth. He especially used three men, all with the name of Bob, to prepare me for the purpose and calling on my life.

The common ingredient that each of these men expressed was the ability to see me with a greater sense of purpose and destiny than I saw myself. They all challenged me to believe in the God of the impossible, and their influence in my life helped to develop my core values.

1) Bob Lund/HFC 1965 - The values of self-discipline and diligence!

Power, Love, Self-Control
Not of Fear

Whatever you do, work heartily, as for the Lord and not for men... (Col. 3:23)

For God gave us a spirit not of fear but of power and love and self-control. (2 Tim. 1:7)

Bob Lund was the Branch Manager of Household Finance Corporation in Lincoln, Nebraska. After getting out of the United States Air Force in August of '64, I spent a short time attending college while working part time without any sense of real direction for my life or Mary's and our marriage. Mary and I married in March of '63 while I was in the service, we got pregnant on our honeymoon (unplanned), and I spent the next sixteen months in Okinawa. In January of '65, our young family of three moved to Lincoln and I began employment at HFC with a starting income of $325 per month. Amazing now to reflect, but we had rent on a furnished apartment, a car payment, and groceries to buy—all on a whopping net income of $145.10 twice a month!

As I began the one year manager's training program with HFC, my goal was to complete the program as soon as possible, knowing that for each three-month segment that I completed, I would receive a salary increase of $20 per month. Little did I realize, I was about to meet one of the most positive, delightful, energetic, and hard-working men that I had ever been around. Up front, I made it clear to Mr. Lund that I needed to get pay increases as fast as I could, and he committed himself to helping me do just that.

Long story short, I completed all twelve months' training in the record time of four months by working long hours night and day plus Saturdays (by choice). In fact, the HFC Regional Office could not process the quarterly segments fast enough, so that by the time I completed the course, the initial $20-per-month raise finally showed

up in my paycheck. What a learning experience for growing in my understanding as to the value of self-discipline
and diligence only for me to realize years later that these
are core qualities that the Apostle Paul would address
in his epistles to the Church. Although Mr. Lund never
expressed his faith in God outwardly, I knew that there
was something unique about this man that was investing greatly into my life. Only after becoming a follower of
Christ, did I realize that Mr. Lund had been mentoring me
in biblical principles that would shape me significantly for
the glory of God. I'm forever grateful!

2) Bob Noyes/pastor-teacher, Christ is King Community
Church (1979-1998) - The Word of God transforms you!

*All Scripture is breathed out by God and profitable for teach-
ing, for reproof, for correction, and for training in righteousness, that the man of God may be complete, equipped for
every good work. (2 Tim. 3:16-17)*

See also: Hebrews 4:12-13 and Psalm 119:105,130.

I met Bob number 2 after moving back to Mary's
hometown of Norfolk, Nebraska, in January of 1979. At
that time, Bob was an associate pastor at the church we
had started attending, and it wasn't long before we struck
up a relationship that was centered around a love for the
Word of God. Bob had a deep commitment to raising what
he referred to as "24/7 disciples of Jesus Christ" which in-
cluded teaching young believers how to meditate on the
Scriptures. This is exactly what I was looking for and what
I needed as a young three-year-old in the Lord. Over the
next several years, Bob and I would share many hours together rejoicing and encouraging one another in what
we were learning through the Word and, specifically, how
I was learning to memorize, meditate on, and apply the

Word of God to my life. Bob, who had become the senior leader of a new church plant that we were a part of, invited me to come on staff as his administrative assistant in 1982. Bob recognized the call of God on my life and made a place for me to grow in my faith, leadership skills, and calling to preach and teach the Word of God. I am eternally grateful for his investment in my life!

3) Bob Swanger/apostle-pastor and spiritual leader (1991-1995) - "The Holy Spirit of God can be trusted!"

"If you love Me, you will keep My commandments. And I will ask the Father, and He will give you another Helper, to be with you forever, even the Spirit of truth, whom the world cannot receive, because it neither sees Him nor knows Him. You know Him, for He dwells with you and will be in you. I will not leave you as orphans; I will come to you." (John 14:15-18)

See also: John 16:13-15.

By the time I met Bob number three, I had already had several very personal encounters with the Third Person of the Godhead, The Holy Spirit. However, I had never been around a leader who walked so intimately with the Holy Spirit, was so sensitive to His voice, and reflected the image of Christ in all that he did. At the time I met Pastor Bob, I was no longer pastoring a church, but selling international airline tickets to ministers, churches, and missionaries as my 'tent-making' job while doing missions in Eastern Europe. Beginning in October of 1991, I was privileged to provide all of Pastor Bob's airline tickets, both domestically and internationally, including coordinating a tour to Israel in '94.

It was through Bob, I began to witness and understand that the very person of God, the Holy Spirit, was living inside of me, and that I could trust Him to be my Helper, Teacher, Guide, and Comforter—the One who convicts me of sin and who empowers me to live the victorious Christian life. That is the very person of the Holy Spirit that led me into all truth and who releases His gifts through me as He wills to strengthen and edify the body of Christ and to minister to a broken and lost world. Bob lived out his life with much integrity and love for the Word of God and the Body of Christ through his intimacy with the Holy Spirit. I believe that it was through brother Bob, and his laying on of hands with prayer, that an unending love for God's people was imparted to me. He was the one who taught me to always see people as God sees them: through His destiny for them rather than through their failures. I believe with my whole heart that it is impossible to do that without an intimate walk with the Holy Spirit!

Cultural Influence in Our Core Values

Grady: From the earliest part of our lives, culture has a powerful influence upon our core values. It includes where we grew up geographically and where and how we were educated. Social and secular media continues to make the world accessible and more connected for each generation. The overall change from a Judeo-Christian societal foundation of values to a post-modern secular value system has had significant impact upon our cultural and individual core values. Furthermore, the religious and faith values given to us by our parents have shaped much of our core values and beliefs. We must each examine and evaluate these influences in the history of our lives to help discover where and how our core values have been formed.

Let's consider our geographical community's influence. Often, we have been significantly unaware of the power these different cultures have held in our lives and their substantial influence on our core values. Some things are obvious such as speech, mannerisms, and certain behaviors. However, there are deeper issues that have infiltrated and affected our foundational core beliefs that derive from our cultural environments.

These deeper influences can include prejudice, attitude, faith, political viewpoint, and much more. How we live is often impacted greatly by the culture we grow up in and, as stated earlier, we often are not aware of this fact at all when it comes to some of the deepest values we have in our inner self. Every social group we are involved in has significant power in the building and establishing of our basic core values.

I grew up in the Midwest. My parents were both factory workers in the aircraft industry, and no one in our immediate family had a college degree. These things had a great impact in how I thought about everything. Many of my values connected directly to these cultural influences. Throughout my lifetime, I have both reacted to and duplicated these influences.

My parents never verbally encouraged or discouraged me from going to college. However, in the wider culture (outside of our strong blue-collar, Midwest mindset) it was becoming a core value for all young people to at least strongly consider getting a degree. For whatever reason, this motivated me to take on a core belief that I needed to go get that degree. There were certainly other influences. However, as I look back and examine my thinking and decision to go to college, I realize that the community value (not my family system) had made a significant impact on me in this regard.

Additionally, going to college would bring into my world many new value possibilities. Educational culture is so powerful in our lives. Our education affects not merely facts and information but values and beliefs! I'm sure we all know that education has this influence. However, we often haven't examined the depth of its impact in how it has shaped (or reshaped) our core values and beliefs.

Another growing influence in how our core values are shaped comes from the culture of social and secular mediums. We are truly living in a global system. It's almost become like the days when the great tower of Babel was being built. Today nearly every culture has contact and influence upon one another. We are all communicating, sharing ideas, and economically dependent upon each other. Today you can travel to almost any country and interact with other cultural value systems. This is shaping us and expanding the possible influences on our core values.

There is a great gap between the Baby Boomers and the Millennial Generation due to these changes. It causes great differences in social and individual core values in society and within the Christ-believing community. This is a challenge that must be embraced to understand the different and changing core values of a generation of young adults. We need to be able to work together to seek what are biblically sound values for us as individuals and as a society.

Our faith and religious environment has significant impact on our belief system. Even within churches and between Christians of varying faiths, we discover an assortment of very different core values. As I grew up in a particular faith culture (denomination), I had certain beliefs and ideas about other faith groups that were not necessarily accurate or healthy. I trusted the social core beliefs about such groups until I could differentiate my ideas as I ventured out into other social contexts (such as college) and discovered that many of my views regarding other faith groups were incorrect.

Furthermore, many of the basic core values regarding

my faith came from the denominational culture I experienced Christ within as a young boy and teen. Over time, in my personal study of Scripture, some of those core beliefs had to be adjusted as I discovered truth that they ignored or interpreted differently from myself and others. Nevertheless, many of the core values regarding my Christian faith and practice still find their roots in the faith system I grew up in. I think I have differentiated some of the values that were based more on tradition and fear than on good biblical hermeneutics.

When searching for your core values don't neglect the cultural values that helped shape your internal/foundational beliefs. They are so subdued and yet powerful in our deepest core values.

CHAPTER EIGHT

WHERE OUR CORE VALUES
NEED TO COME FROM

A Biblical Foundation of Truth

One critical question is: Where do we go with confidence to find the right core values? Remember, we all have core values. From our earliest moments in life, we began to gather them through the relationships, environments, and experiences we have. As we become teens and begin our entry into adulthood, many of our core values are challenged by new relationships, environments, and experiences. This is true for everyone, not just Christians.

As we begin to face the challenges that confront our core beliefs, we need to know where we can go to find truth. Non-Christians may think they have many options in which to find truth—many sources, all of their choosing. However, these non-biblical sources of truth really come from the same foundational core value—pride or self-love. Therefore, their truth is based on the lie that believes we can find value, worth, and truth from ourselves or human knowledge. These non-biblical sources of truth lead us to the same dead end!

There is a source of truth that comes from the Creator of humankind—the Bible. However, one must place their faith in the reality that God's Word is the true source of truth. Everything we are presenting to you about Core

Values depends on this one thing—that you believe the Bible, God's Word, as the source of all truth. If you can't believe this one thing the process will not bring life to you. The Bible is our source of truth. It is the Word of God we compare and measure our core values against to determine what is right and what is life giving.

In 2 Timothy, we find our hope and what we must believe if we are to pursue the process of developing life-giving core values.

> All Scripture is breathed out by God and profitable for teaching, for reproof, for correction, and for training in righteousness, that the man of God may be complete, equipped for every good work. (2 Tim. 3:16-17)

These God-given words of truth must be pursued and believed if one is to experience profit and the ability to confidently establish core values that will lead us into a life worth living.

After all his failures, King David found in God's Word the truth and values he needed to overcome his pride and his weakness. He states in Psalms:

> Oh how I love Your law! It is my meditation all the day. Your commandment makes me wiser than my enemies, for it is ever with me. I have more understanding than all my teachers, for Your testimonies are my meditation. I understand more than the aged, for I keep Your precepts. I hold back my feet from every evil way, in order to keep Your word. I do not turn aside from Your rules, for You have taught me. How sweet are Your words to my taste, sweeter than honey to my mouth! Through Your precepts I get understanding; therefore I hate every false way. (Ps. 119:97-104)

David, through years of seeking God's truth and Spirit, had come to a place of knowing and establishing his core values with confidence and was experiencing a better life; a life he had been created to live. It's no different for you and me! Like David, we can live in the process of finding who we are and what we need to believe so we can experience life in the way God intended for us. Furthermore— and this is important—we can do this during any circumstance, crisis, or challenge the enemy and life can throw at us.

From a Spirit of God's Grace

We need to clarify that we are not suggesting that having mere knowledge of God's truth from His Word is the way to find and experience life in Him. In other words, we are not offering you a life of religious devotion to principles and rules. It's not just a goal of knowing truth and obeying the precepts of God in pursuit of becoming like God—that just reverts to living under the curse. Without understanding His love and grace, the truth of God's Word doesn't lead us to His best for us. It just leads us into religion, and there is little life in that.

Jesus came with grace and truth. He came to earth to show us this very reality. The Sadducees and Pharisees knew the Word of Truth. However, they didn't know the greatest and foremost truth that He is love! This reality of God as love is a foundational core value we must come to understand. If we don't, we will only find religion like the men and women who nailed Jesus to a cross. He is truth; however, He is also love!

The Apostle Paul seemed to have reshaped all his core values throughout his life in Christ. He knew the law of the Old Testament. Throughout his Epistles, he makes clear that he knew the law and he obeyed the law, but until he met Jesus on the road to Damascus, he was a lost man. His core values had not been touched by the love of God and the true purpose of God's law that was meant to bring life, not bondage.

The core value of reli-
gion is self-righteousness. In
Philippians 3, Paul expresses
that if anyone could proclaim

The core value of religion is self-righteousness.

self-righteousness, it was him. He was the best of the best
when it came to having the right knowledge and obeying
the truth. However, he goes on to proclaim:

> For we are the circumcision, who worship by the Spirit of God
> and glory in Christ Jesus and put no confidence in the flesh—
> though I myself have reason for confidence in the flesh also.
> If anyone else thinks he has reason for confidence in the
> flesh, I have more. (Phil. 3:3-4)

A few verses later, he continues:

> Indeed, I count everything as loss because of the surpassing
> worth of knowing Christ Jesus my Lord. For His sake I have
> suffered the loss of all things and count them as rubbish, in
> order that I may gain Christ and be found in Him, not having
> a righteousness of my own that comes from the law, but that
> which comes through faith in Christ, the righteousness from
> God that depends on faith— (Phil. 3:8-9)

So, knowing truth and obeying the rules from just our
own strength and will is not enough. Every core value we
establish should be connected to the truth of His Word.
However, it must also stand on the reality of who Christ is,
and that reality is that He is love.

For example, we believe God gave us the gift of
Sabbath. From Creation on, God wanted us to take time
from our work to give ourselves fully to relationship with
Him and one another. We won't go into all this entails
here, but Sabbath was to be a core value for us to believe
and live out so that we might have a better life in Him

However, the religious take that truth and turn it into
something that brings burden and oppression instead of

life. Obeying the truth and gift of Sabbath without understanding what the Spirit of God's true purpose and intention is for Sabbath leaves us empty and lifeless.

Furthermore, like the religious leaders and teachers
in Christ's time on Earth, we create and follow God from
a core value of *self-righteousness* and not from a place
of God's powerful and loving righteousness. When establishing our core values, they must be built from the
truth and the Spirit from which that truth has been giv-
en to us. Remember, Jesus came *"full of grace and truth"*
(John 1:14b). John goes on to state, *"For the law was given
through Moses; grace and truth came through Jesus Christ"*
(John 1:17).

This is critical to understand. Our core values are not
established apart from the reality of God's love and grace
for us and all humankind! We must know that the foundation of all true and life-giving core values rest on the
reality that our life, hope, righteousness, and ministry—
everything draws its full value and life from the grace and
love of God. Without this, we are no different than the
Sadducees and Pharisees of old!

Therefore, it is the foundational principle, the core value that all others must rest upon, that the Lord Jesus Christ
is the beginning and end of our righteousness. Without
this basic belief in His full work of grace and love for us,
our salvation and continued conversion, we will only create a to-do list of values that will lead us into a system of
religious bondage. A bondage that rests upon the lie that
we must "be god" was the lie offered to Adam and Eve and
is still being whispered into our lives as the way to life.

This can be tricky. We can take a principle of God's Word,
like tithing, and under the curse of seeking self-righteousness, find ourselves doing what seems right but, in reality,
is only an exercise of religious bondage and a dangerous

pursuit of self-righteousness. However, understanding the true gift of God's desire for us to experience giving from a place of putting our full faith in Him as our loving provider, we can become cheerful givers that give abundantly out of gratefulness instead of law and obligation.

So, our core values come not only from the written principles in the Word of God but from the full truth that sets upon the foundation and reality that they must flow from the truth of God's love and gift of righteousness through Jesus Christ. It is in and through this relational existence with God we live out the core values we find in the Bible. It is not built upon the letter of the law but upon the Spirit of the truth through the gift of Christ's grace gift to us from His death on the cross and His resurrection over the curse of death, both now and eternally.

As you search the Scripture for the core values God has given us, be sure to pursue them in the reality that we are sons and daughters of a loving and relational Father, Son, and Holy Spirit. We are stewards of all God is and has, but we are not or cannot be god by our own goodness, obedience, and false hope of obtaining our own righteousness. This basic core belief is the first step toward building and establishing our core values that will help us experience a victorious life in Him.

CHAPTER NINE

THE POWER OF CORE VALUES

What I realized on the journey of discovering, examining, and establishing core values is the powerful reality that when I have clearly and intentionally established a core value such as, "I will believe and live in the reality that I am a son of God," I begin to experience and live in that reality and continue in it. In other words, I start experiencing change and victory in particular areas of my life when I have clearly, specifically, and intentionally established and clarified a core value.

When Sandy and I were engaged to be married, we discussed and created a specific core value that we would never entertain the thought or possibility of divorce in our future marriage, as I mentioned previously. We determined it would never be an option for us. We verbalized it often and to others in our families (mine especially). We established this because divorce had been a significant part of my family system, and we wanted no part of it. Clearly, we understood the damage it brought with it, and we had a healthy fear of it getting a foothold in our marriage. Somehow, we knew (not intentionally at first) that we needed to establish this core value in our marriage relationship. Establishing this value so clearly from the beginning in our marriage allowed us to have victory over even entertaining the thought that divorce was an option for us. We discovered that in this one act of being intentional in the establishment of a core value, it gave us great strength to keep our marriage vow of "to death do us part."

Establishing clear, specific, and thoughtful core values provide great power in our ability to live out the values we believe in. When I clearly stated and believed that I would place a higher value on my family than my ministry, it better enabled me to do it and not fail in this personal arena of my family life. It wasn't that I didn't mess up occasionally, but it did help me when I messed up, to quickly adjust and return to the right path. More often, it helped me to make correct and healthy decisions so that failure wasn't commonplace.

I have experienced this in many areas of my life. Because of engaging in the process of developing my core values, I have been able to walk in victory and health in many areas of my life and ministry. I have seen it be extremely helpful in others' lives as well. Establishing your core values is inviting the power of God's truth to tear down unhealthy strongholds and create places of great strength to bring life to you.

Every individual believer has the power to intentionally enter into and live in the process of renewing our minds by creating and establishing the core values of a son or daughter of our Father in heaven. If you will engage purposely in this adventure and discipline, you will experience a much greater level of victory! We can take dominion over the enemy's powerful lies in our lives by trading the old lies that keep us captive, even as believers, for God's truths that bring life.

I believe 2 Corinthians 10 speaks to this reality and process:

For though we walk in the flesh, we are not waging war according to the flesh. For the weapons of our warfare are not of the flesh but have divine power to destroy strongholds. We destroy arguments and every lofty opinion raised against the knowledge of God, and take every thought captive to obey Christ, being ready to punish every disobedience, when your obedience is complete. (2 Cor. 10:3-6)

Do you want to live in complete obedience to Christ, with power to recognize wrong thoughts and being able to take captive the lies of your old self? Do you want to walk in the spirit and not in the flesh? Having the right core values is a powerful weapon for winning this battle! To know the truth and apply it in your life where once a lie resided is not just something that happens mystically. It happens when we destroy these lies by clearly knowing and establishing the truth in our minds and hearts!

It isn't just Satan that offers us lies to live by. Those who haven't established true core beliefs based on God's Word and Spirit operate in the power of wrong core values or lies. Paul speaks to this in Colossians 2:

For I want you to know how great a struggle I have for you and for those at Laodicea and for all who have not seen me face to face, that their hearts may be encouraged, being knit together in love, to reach all the riches of full assurance of understanding and the knowledge of God's mystery, which is Christ, in whom are hidden all the treasures of wisdom and knowledge. I say this in order that no one may delude you with plausible arguments. (Col. 2:1-4)

How often have *"plausible arguments"* (part truth, part lie) ruled and messed up our lives? I believe part of the hidden *"treasures of wisdom and knowledge"* offered to us in Christ are core values that are completely built on His truth.

Isn't it interesting that Paul mentions his concern for the believers at Laodicea? Revelation 3:14-22 reveals that these believers had a significant problem with being luke-warm. Verse 17 suggests they had placed some of their core belief in a plausible argument!

> *"For you say, I am rich, I have prospered, and I need nothing, not realizing that you are wretched, pitiable, poor, blind, and naked." (Rev. 3:17)*

The facts may have been that in some way they were rich and in need of little. Perhaps, like most of us today, they were very capable of taking care of themselves without much help from God. However, they were blinded to the full truth of their condition. They were living a life of pursuing self-righteousness, seeking personal ownership of their lives without being aware of their lack of living in the fullness of faith in Christ's love and provision.

James 5:7-11 shares some significant core values that a believer should seek and live by so that he or she can remain as steadfast as Job through his intense season of suffering and confusion. With true biblical values established and obeyed, one can live through all the enemy's attacks that seek to kill and destroy us. If we do not know what to believe and value, we will not be steadfast and will be unable to defeat the enemy's schemes. This is the power of having and living in biblical core values.

Jesus offers us a perfect example during His time on earth of the power of having solid biblical core values and beliefs. Matthew 4:1-11 says after His baptism, *"Then Jesus was led up by the Spirit into the wilderness to be tempted by the devil"* (vs. 1). Here, after forty days of fasting food and water, Jesus is tired and weary and about to face the greatest temptation a human had ever been confronted with.

Satan offers some plausible situations to Jesus. First, "If You are the Son of God, command these stones to become loaves of bread" (vs. 3).

But Jesus answered, "It is written, '"Man shall not live by bread alone, but by every word that comes from the mouth of God'" (vs. 4). And with those few words, Jesus defeated Satan's scheme. Why? It was because Jesus had discernment. He knew truth, and this Scripture was established in His mind and heart. It was a core belief and value for Jesus.

Jesus defeated Satan's temptations two more times with the same counterattack—truth. He knew the Word of His Father. Jesus had established these sound and true words in His mind and heart and remained steadfast even during physical and emotional exhaustion. Having these core values firmly in His life, He could overcome Satan's formidable temptations.

The power of establishing sound biblical core values helps us achieve victory over many weaknesses and ongoing sins in our lives. When we

> *...establishing sound biblical core values helps us achieve victory over weaknesses and sins...*

have clearly become aware of what we know and believe to be true in Christ through His Word and example we can rebut the temptations and plausible arguments Satan offers us in our weakest moments.

SECTION FOUR:

Entering the Process

CHAPTER TEN

BEING INTENTIONAL IN FOLLOWING CHRIST

Discovering, creating, and developing biblical core values must be part of the process of growing as a disciple of Jesus Christ. It is not merely a work of our flesh. It must be done in the reality of a living relationship with the Father, Son, and Holy Spirit. Like Jesus, we must learn to live in communion with the Father, listening for His voice and leading.

Of course, knowing and obeying Scripture is a significant element of the process. However, we must also learn to listen for whatever the Spirit might need to speak to us to truly establish and live in *our* sound, life-giving core values. Ultimately, it's about becoming a real disciple—a follower of Christ—not merely a discipline of getting the right knowledge in place (Gnosticism). It's about having a daily relationship with the Lord as a son or daughter of the Father. It isn't simply creating and becoming obedient to a list of good things to do, that's law keeping. The Pharisees did that, and they missed the Messiah!

In Mark 10:17-22 we read the story of the *Rich Young Ruler*. He wanted to follow Christ and be a true disciple, and he thought he was equipped to do so. He had good core values and had kept the law diligently. However, Jesus spoke to him regarding the one thing he lacked—the key core value he had not yet discovered. Jesus offered him the way, the value he could obey in order to move from law keeper to disciple. *"'You lack one thing: go, sell all that you have and give to the poor, and you will have treasure in heaven; and come, follow Me'"* (Mark 10:21).

If we are to experience the power of discovering and engaging in life-giving core values, we will have to be intentional in our pursuit of whatever God reveals to us. We need to take it one core value at a time. This requires a discipline (especially at the beginning) of engaging our thinking toward the practical focus of engaging the process. However, to truly experience and live in the core values we establish, we must be intentional in our discipleship, our following of Christ in a daily relational focus on Him. In my pursuit of discovering, redefining, and establishing life-giving core values, I find it often comes one step at a time. Frequently, it is an ongoing experience that changes me to the core! As I grew in defining and establishing my core value of self (see Chapter Twelve), I went on a journey of "next steps." Making a list of biblical core values was just a part of the process. Maturing in my personal relationship with the Lord, hearing His Holy Spirit, and having times of personal devotion were and are so much at the center of the process. So, as I grow in identifying and developing great core values, I am advancing in my relationship with the Father, Son, and Holy Spirit. I am becoming a disciple, a follower of Jesus. This is the real reward.

In my journey to define my core values of "self," God led me to see and begin to believe that I was more than His redeemed slave. He helped me begin to see that I was His son. When I really started the journey to believe this in my heart, my first step was to say, "I am one of His sons," but at the same time I thought, "But, I'm not His best son."

Then, as I continued my journey, I began to see the next step was to believe that I was His favorite son—loved 100 percent.

After this, the next development in the process was to see that the Lord wanted me to be His friend. The process continues even today, years later. There always seems to be a next step of growth and change and my core value of self continues to grow and bring more truth and life to me! So, I have become intentional in looking for and taking the next steps. This didn't come from merely writing down and following a core value statement. It becomes life as I intentionally seek to follow Jesus relationally.

When I married Sandy, I professed vows to her that I meant, but honestly, I didn't fully understand the depth of these vows in the context of our life together. However, over 38 plus years of marriage I have learned (and am still learning) what those vows really meant and how to apply them to our daily relationship together. I have had to be intentional in exploring and making effort to learn what my marriage vows really mean in the reality of our relationship together. The same is true for anyone who wants to establish and experience the power and life that can come from knowing and intentionally practicing the core values God has led us to.

Therefore, we must be intentional in the practical, thinking, and activity aspect of the process and we must

> *Being intentional to engage in a daily, focused relationship with the Lord is a must!*

also be intentional in the relational and devotional aspect of growing as a disciple of Christ. So, we invite you to determine to dedicate yourself to be, and remain, intentional to this whole process. If you will, we can guarantee life-giving results.

Being intentional to engage in a daily, focused

relationship with the Lord is a must! Continue to contemplate and work out on paper the different areas of developing and establishing our core values. This is also not an option but a requirement if we want to experience a true discovery and establishment of our core values. It is the entering of a discipline and relationship with God that requires the involvement of mind, soul, and spirit. We invite you to take the next step in seeking to discover, define, and establish life-giving core values that will keep you growing as a true follower and disciple of Jesus Christ.

CHAPTER ELEVEN

DIFFERENT APPROACHES

Relationships

Dick and I thought about our own journeys as we began to dialogue about how we should pursue helping others discover and develop healthy, biblical core values (at that time, men were our focus). As we talked, we realized that most core values were built within relationships.

We have coached and mentored men toward discovering and identifying the importance of biblical core values in their roles as sons, husbands, fathers, men in God's community of believers, and men of God in the world. We have found these areas cover almost every variety of relationship. If men could figure out healthy, godly core values within these different areas of relationships, great things would happen. Dick had a group of young men in this process already.

Dick: About the same time, we started dialoguing about the issues surrounding core values in our lives, I was also challenging a group of younger men to "come away to a quiet place" to learn how to recognize God's voice. During this season, the Holy Spirit began speaking to me about the importance of helping my brothers understand their distinctive roles and relationships as being ordained by our Creator. Although this group began with just three men, it wasn't long before it expanded to eight. Obviously, the hand of God was resting upon it.

Without realizing what was going on, Mary and I had been experiencing the leading of the Holy Spirit for several years regarding how we would care for our parents in their later years so that they could enjoy those last years and then pass on into eternity with dignity. We had made some core value decisions as a son and daughter that would make it possible for us to be available to provide that end-of-life care for our parents.

As a result of this process, I had begun to identify and examine every role and relationship area God had given me as a man. How exciting it was to study the Scriptures and seek the Lord for insight and understanding as to my God-ordained responsibilities. As relational issues arose in the lives of the men I was mentoring, I found myself challenging them to examine what core values they were operating out of in those relationships.

> *They didn't even know there were other values available that would bring freedom...*

It was eye-opening, and it wasn't long before Grady and I began to incorporate identifying these roles as sons, husbands, fathers, men of God in the community of believers, and men of God in the world into our teaching material.

For the past decade, we have been inviting and helping men discover and establish core values in these different areas of their life relationships. Men have been able to enter this life-changing process, rebuilding their values regarding all the relationships they have according to God's plan for living life in Him.

Topical

Grady: Another way to explore and establish core values is by topic. Sandy and I had the opportunity to teach parenting classes at a local pregnancy center. She does most of the classes, but I help her with a couple of the topics. One of the topics I help with is finances. As we began to teach these mostly single and non-Christian, expectant moms and dads about money, it became clear that they had very different core values than are offered from God's Word. Their thinking about money was dramatically different from God's plan and principles.

After revealing their current cultural values about money, we introduced them to a whole new paradigm about God's view of it. It was so exciting to see the transformation in their thinking about money. They didn't even know there were other values available that would bring freedom from the weight of their secular core ideas about finances.

We began to help them discover the dangerous and unhealthy values our culture has about money. As we exposed the wrong principles and fallacies with these values and expressed the simple but life-giving ideals of biblical truths about money, we saw the "light" come on in their minds. For many, it was the first time they could have hope about their future with money.

We have explored and experienced many topics about our core values. These topics can be in all areas of our lives. Spiritual realms, such as our value of God's Word, can be explored and established. Is the Bible truly His Divine Word to us? Our foundation regarding this value is found in 2 Timothy:

All Scripture is breathed out by God and profitable for teaching, for reproof, for correction, and for training in righteousness, that the man of God may be complete, equipped for every good work. (2 Tim. 3:16-17)

So, we are solid in our belief about the Bible being God's inerrant word to humankind.

Practical and diverse areas such as money, parenting, career, and friendship can all be examined and established clearly in our lives. The process we are about to introduce can work for either the relational or topical approach. We have found that both are helpful and recommend that people do both.

CHAPTER TWELVE

THE FIRST RELATIONAL FOUNDATION OF CORE VALUES: THE IDENTITY OF OUR TRUE SELVES

If you choose to delve into the journey of discovering and intentionally establishing biblical, life-giving core values, the best, but most difficult, place to begin is with figuring out your self-identity. Who am I? This seems to be the most important question every human being needs and wants answered during their lifetime. We have been on that journey and have discovered more of the reality that we are sons of the Living God. He values us and wants us to know who we are considering His plan for each of

> *...the best, but most difficult, place to begin is with figuring out your self-identity.*

us since we were in our mother's womb. Here are some reflections of our journey toward discovering and establishing our core value of self.

Discovering Your Identity as a Son

Dick: Every human being seems to experience the journey of trying to figure out their identity or who they are. As a boy, and one of the smaller kids in my age group, I was always trying to prove that I could compete with those who were sometimes much bigger than me. Too small for football, I discovered that my size didn't pose near the hindrances in baseball, so at a young age, I decided that would be my sport. I was certainly an overachiever, but the hard work and hours of practice paid off, especially on the defensive side of the ball as I discovered that my hard work ethic and quick reflexes caught the coach's eyes.

This continued through my military service and on into my adult business career. Even though I received recognition by winning sales contests and promotion into management positions, I was always looking for a way to prove that I had worth and value. I even spent a season in business as a sales motivational speaker not only to make a living for my family, but deep down trying to prove to myself that I was "somebody." Of course, with all the wounds from childhood and generational curses, such as alcohol, gambling, immorality, and impure thought life that were operating in me, I could never fill that void in my life.

After several near-death experiences while intoxicated in the early to mid-seventies, I realized that I hated the hypocrite that I looked at every morning in the mirror. Initially, this only led to endless, unkept promises to Mary and attempts to fix my own life and then to thoughts of suicide that, fortunately, I never mustered up the courage to follow through with. There were times when I attempted to negotiate with God, such as after I had passed out drunk at the wheel and drove underneath a semi-trailer in Dallas, Texas. I ended up in Parkland Hospital saying something like, "God, if You'll let me live, I'll straighten out." Of course, that only lasted until I was back on my feet, back at work, and facing the next stress-filled situation. Then through some amazingly unusual circumstance, the company that I was working for decided to promote me and move us to the Kansas City area. Little did I know that God was about to sneak up on me. That was when we bought some acreage in the country directly across from a pastor who was filled with the unconditional love of God and preached the Word of God with power and authority.

Six months later, after watching Pastor Fred Powell coming in and out of his home with such joy in his heart, singing at the top of his lungs, I finally said to Mary that we should visit his church, and she readily agreed. It was in January of 1976 when we visited Pisgah Baptist Church for the first time. Pastor Powell preached the gospel with such authority, and it was as if he knew everything about me. I was under such deep conviction that I couldn't wait to get out of that building! I managed to make it to the car only to discover that all three of our children absolutely loved what they had just experienced. "Let's come back here again!" they were saying in unison.

I kept my only thought to myself, "Over my dead body!"

I stand in awe as to how the Holy Spirit works to draw us to this loving Heavenly Father who will move heaven, and earth to bring us to Himself. By the following Sunday, I had forgotten all about what had happened in our car after the previous Sunday's worship service. I met with no resistance, in fact just the opposite, when I suggested once again that we should visit Pastor Powell's church.

My life was about to be changed forever! This time, as the Word of God was preached with such authority, my heart was deeply convicted that I was a sinner and that Christ had died for me. My entire sin debt had already been paid on Calvary, and I knew He would forgive me and allow me to experience a new life in Christ! The invitation was given to receive Christ as my Lord and Savior, and I found myself collapsed at the altar crying my heart out to this loving Father who loved me so much that He chose to send Jesus to die on my behalf that I might have eternal life! I got up from that altar a changed man—filled with the joy of the Lord and feeling so cleansed and free.

Over the next several months I couldn't read the Word of God enough. I discovered what the Apostle Paul meant

when he wrote to the Corinthian believers as recorded in
2 Corinthians 5:17, *"Therefore, if anyone is in Christ, he is a
new creation; old things have passed away; behold, all things
have become new."* The Scriptures were coming alive to
me almost daily. I was truly experiencing a honeymoon
with this One who died for me and was revealing a new
dimension of the Father's love each day.

In the midst of this amazing journey that I found myself on, the insurance company that I was working for was
going through huge changes, and it meant frequently fly-
ing into Dallas for meetings. I left one meeting with great
frustration and anger only to find myself ordering and
drinking several alcoholic beverages on the flight home.
Keep in mind that I had lived the past two months since
coming to Christ without drinking any alcohol. Upon war-
rival in Kansas City, I proceeded to the bar across from my
office and continued to drink until closing.

Miraculously, I arrived home in this drunken condition
after 2:30 a.m. only to have Mary meet me at the door. I
was about to encounter this God that I barely knew in a
way that I couldn't have imagined. As Mary met me at the
door, God supernaturally imposed the following words on
her forehead. "I knew that it was too good to last." With
a saddened countenance, Mary didn't say a word to me
but just looked me in the eyes with a broken heart. In my
drunken stupor, I saw the pain in my beloved wife's heart
for the first time. After innumerable promises repeatedly
broken, Mary had finally had a glimmer of hope that was
crushed by my failure once again. Without speaking, Mary
turned around and went back to bed.

I was devastated by the pain that I had just witnessed in
Mary's eyes and by those words that I had seen across her
forehead: *"I knew that it was too good to last."* Immediately,
I went down into our family room and fell on the floor in

front of our sofa crying out to God saying, "If you are really there, God, help me!"

I heard an audible response. "Dick, I know that you mean it, and you don't have to worry anymore." Overwhelmed with a sense of His presence and love, I immediately fell asleep on the sofa. Only a few days later while spending time early one morning reading Scripture, I heard that still small voice say, "I want you to take all the alcohol in the house and throw it away; you won't need it anymore." Space doesn't allow for me to share the hundreds of times that I've heard the Lord refer to me as "son" as He is about to speak something very important into my spirit. Several years ago, when I was attending a conference about understanding that we are sons of God, I heard my Heavenly Father say to me, "Son, you've known you were My son since the day you were saved!" to which I was overcome to the point of tears with great joy, peace, and contentment. This is my true identity—I am His son. This is where my value comes from, and it is the foundation of who we are.

A Very Different Journey Toward Discovering My True Self

Grady: For me, it was January 1996. I was in Toronto, Canada, visiting what has been labeled the "Toronto Blessing." I went for several reasons. As a pastor, you often must investigate the things that are having an impact on those in your care. The "Toronto Blessing" was having an impact within my church and within the entire church world, so I wanted to check it out for myself. I was also doing some research for my Master's program. And there was one more reason—I was spiritually dry at the time and was hoping for some rejuvenation for myself.

During one of the services, God did touch me—simply and powerfully. Hundreds of people were lying all over the floor around me after they had been prayed for by the leaders. I was the only one still standing. As I stood amongst the multitude, I felt such emptiness, and I really wanted to hear something from the Lord. I was also tired, and since everyone else was on the floor, I decided to just lie down on the floor. As soon as my head touched the floor, I began to hear the Lord speak to me, clearly and specifically.

God revealed to me that I had the heart of an orphan. He exposed some deep, hidden areas in my heart and subconsciousness. At that moment, He reminded me of what my mom had told me years ago about my birth father and how he had left us a few months after I was born. Although I hadn't any conscious anger or hurt from this fact, He allowed me to see that it had deeply impacted my entire being and my deepest core value of how I saw myself. For the first time in my life I began to think about what I knew was theologically true—I am His son! I'm not sure how long I stayed on the floor, but it seemed like hours.

At the age of 39, I was just beginning to become truly aware of my identity issues —the most important core value in my life. Understanding was given to me, for the first time, of the foundational core value of God's love for me. It was in total opposition to the lie of pride which said that if I accepted self-love as the basis of belief for where my value comes from, I could "be like God."

What if it really were true that God loved me as a son, and His love for me was a hundred percent all the time? This core value that I was working on was at the deepest hub of my life. All I believed about God and myself hung in the balance of understanding who I truly am. The next several years became a significant journey to discover, rethink, and search the Word of God. Along with seeking others' input and meditating, I finally established the most important core value ever made in my life.

It was only a few months before the airport discussion with Dick that I established in my mind and heart once and for all: *I am a son of the most-high God, and He is my Father!* This new core value changed my life forever. After establishing this, God began to open up a new life for me. At this point, I discovered the next season for my life and ministry.

Have you established the core value of self? Few people realize that they have always had a core value of self! The truth is that we were all born with the belief that we must find and establish love of self (pride) as our basic self-identity. This core value leads us away from God's truth, and it causes us (and the world around us) to establish most of our core values upon this foundational error.

Do you know the true love and value God places upon you and His relationship with you? Understanding this will open up many other deep

> *Do you know the true love and value God places upon you and His relationship with you?*

core value possibilities. Here is a list of some of the core values I have established in my life after discovering and believing my core value of self:

- God truly is *love*, and He loves me 100 percent all the time.
- I do not have to perform (do anything) for God to gain His value and love.
- My ministry is an act of thankfulness and gratefulness for His love for me.
- I don't have to find my value and love from humankind.
- I will seek to love God with all my mind, heart, and soul.
- I will seek to love others because He loves me.

- My Father is my provider in all things such as money, time, ministry opportunity, and fruit. I believe and will place my trust in God.
- I will be free from envy in my relationship with others.
- I will be willing to be a "fool for Christ."

For both of us, this has been the most significant core value to explore and discover what the Father, Son, and Holy Spirit have revealed to us in the Scriptures. What is amazing is that we know the words, and we can quote the many places in the Word that express our sonship; yet, we struggle so to believe it fully for ourselves. It was only when we intentionally focused and worked on moving past knowledge toward a real believing faith that we have been able to clearly establish and begin to live from the core value that we were all created to be sons and daughters of the living God and Father. We encourage you to take our challenge to go on the journey of establishing your core value of self in the life-giving reality of God's love for you as his son or daughter.

CHAPTER THIRTEEN

THE PROCESS

We want to introduce you to the process we have used and have led others through to develop and establish life-giving core values. From the beginning, our goal was to make it as simple as possible to start and finish this journey. So, first, we want to introduce you to the concept and the value of the process, and then we will get more specific and help guide you through the process.

We have created the chart on the next page to show the major steps or flow of the process. This is a journey that is

> *For us, it's more of a way to live than a formula, and it is practical.*

intended to be taken over and over for the rest of our lives as we grow in Christ. For us, it's more of a way to live than a formula, and it is practical. It has proven helpful to discover past and current core values, search the Scriptures to see if they are biblical or built on untruths, and finally, to guide one into creating life-giving core values that are based on the reality of God's Word, grace and truth.

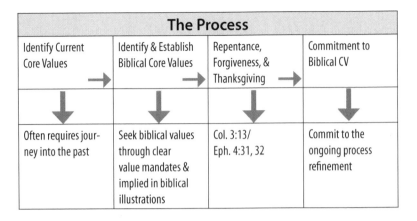

The Process			
Identify Current Core Values →	Identify & Establish Biblical Core Values →	Repentance, Forgiveness, & Thanksgiving →	Commitment to Biblical CV
↓	↓	↓	↓
Often requires journey into the past	Seek biblical values through clear value mandates & implied in biblical illustrations	Col. 3:13/ Eph. 4:31, 32	Commit to the ongoing process refinement

*see Appendix: A

Four Steps in the Process:

Step One: Identity the values in your life already. Remember, this can be approached by looking through relationship roles or topically. We suggest you just take one at a time. The best and simplest way to begin is to ask the Holy Spirit to guide you in selecting the core value you want to discover and journey with through the process. For example, you may want to choose the topic of money and begin to explore what you think you believe about money. We will get more specific later. It will take some time for this first step, and new things may come to mind as you work through the process.

Step Two: After identifying most of your current core values, begin the process of searching the Scriptures to discover what they say about your area of values. So, if your topic is money, we invite you to search the Scriptures and all they say about money. Dick has shared how he and Mary went through these first two steps in their journey. Again, this step can take some time. However, there are many study tools that can help you through this part of the process. The primary tool available to help in this task is an exhaustive/analytical Bible concordance.

After Step Two, you will see where you stand! How do your current core values align with Scripture? In the comparison, you will most likely find opposing values. This is where it becomes life changing because now you must choose what you will believe.

Through thoughtful, honest consideration, you've discovered that you have had a belief from the beginning that debt was not a problem—even though you've been miserable with the debt that weighs you down. As you have examined debt in light of the Word of God, you see that it reveals that debt is a trap to steal your freedom. What will you do?

Step Three: Ask for forgiveness and repent for believing and living under the old core value of this world. This is not merely an intellectual pursuit; it is very much a spiritual journey.

You may also have exposed some vows and strongholds that you have made in the past. There may be others who were a part of your vow that you need to forgive. This step may be difficult, and you may need help in accomplishing it. However, new core values can't be established if these things are not dealt with.

You may need to ask for personal forgiveness for making a foolish vow and believing a lie from the enemy as well. This is like when I made the vow that I wouldn't let anyone humiliate me! I not only needed to forgive my stepfather, but I needed to ask God to forgive me for making a foolish vow as an 8-year-old boy. I also had to renounce the vow. After that, I could have thankfulness in my heart for my dad and for myself, and joy began to replace anger, fear, and hurt in my heart. We will look at this in more detail in Chapter Seventeen.

Step Four: The final step is to proclaim and establish your new biblically-sound core value that declares, "I will live free from debt." Now, like never before, you will be able to proceed to live out this freeing truth in your life. It may take some time (even years), but now you are on the road to life in the area of money. It is a launching pad toward practical and spiritual growth and success in a particular area of your life.

After going through this process once, you will hopefully be on your way to exploring more core values. You will begin to renew your mind with what is true, experiencing more and more the life God created you to have in Him. If you are like us, you will begin to live in the process. We believe it is part of the process of being a growing disciple of Jesus Christ!

CHAPTER FOURTEEN

LIVING IN THE PROCESS OF CREATING AND DEVELOPING CORE VALUES

Grady: It has been 37 years now on this journey. I continue to explore the depths of my mind, emotions, and heart—seeking to establish the core values God created in me. In my ongoing relationship with Him, I want to become fully what He created me to be, even though I live in this fallen world. I am very deliberate in staying on this journey of discovering and establishing my core values as a son of God. Now, like eating food, it is just an ongoing part of my life. Through this intentional process, it still amazes me that I keep discovering many deep issues in my heart that God wants to reveal and refine in my life.

Earlier, I wrote that one of the core values I have established is that "I will be a fool for Christ." This value evolved for me through the yearly ministry I help lead which offers a sabbatical retreat for men. It has become a significant, annual experience for many men we relate to. We try to create an opportunity for men to take several days to seek God by quieting themselves and just learning to listen for Him to speak to their hearts.

For Dick and me, it really isn't a Sabbath. We are investing our thoughts and attention toward creating an atmosphere for the others to experience a true Sabbath. However, I have used it as an opportunity to take some time to revisit my core values and ask the Lord to reveal the next heart issue I need to deal with in my life. He has been so faithful to speak to me each year.

The first year, I specifically asked the Lord to give me a new value to work on. He led me into a journey of mind and heart that would bring great healing into an area of my life I didn't even know was broken.

During the retreat, I found a few hours for some quiet, listening time with the Lord. I asked the Lord a question

> *Lord, what is one thing You would have me deal with in my heart for the next year?*

that has now become an annual occurrence for me. The question was, "Lord, what is one thing You would have me deal with in my heart for the next year?" The question was unplanned; it just came out of my thoughts.

The Spirit answered me with one word, "humiliation." I think I was expecting more than a word, but that was His initial answer. With that one word, I began a voyage that would take me a year to complete. Over the next few months, I spent many hours exploring my past, thinking, listening, studying Scripture, and contemplating the word *humiliation*. It was a life-changing journey that revealed a deeply broken part of my heart and life. It revealed an unhealthy core value that had ruled a significant part of my life, and I didn't even know it was there, substantially controlling many of my daily life actions and decisions.

It was from this intense journey that I created the new core value that "I will be a fool for Christ." No more would my fear of humiliation keep me from trusting God and following His direction each day of my life. It allowed me to break a powerful lie I had placed my faith in for many years in my life. It helped me understand an area of frustration that had cluttered my life for years and kept me bound up and controlled by an invisible lie. In this area of my life, I am now finding more freedom to live as God intended for me to live. This is the power of discovering the wrong core values, taking them captive, and destroying their place in my life; and then establishing new, biblical, God-centered values that I was created to live by.

I continue to stay in the process. It has become a part of my mindset to view life, circumstances, and sin issues through the lens of my core value process. I want to clearly know and be able to quickly and readily establish what I believe in every area of my life upon God's Word and principles. I am amazed how often, in a momentary situation, a core value statement comes to my consciousness and helps me know how to respond and make a quick decision.

Furthermore, when I find myself in a situation that demands a response and I'm confused or I quickly make an uninformed or unhealthy choice or decision, I often realize that I need to intentionally go into my core value process. At the next opportune time I will go through the process. This will enable me to be equipped to make a better response or decision. It still amazes me after all these years of processing and establishing clear core values how often I find myself at a crisis of belief in some situation. However, I don't panic now, I just realize that when this happens it is an opportunity to grow and conquer another area of weakness in my life. It's a key element in my discipleship growing lifestyle.

Dick and I continue to recognize that this process of discovering, evaluating, and establishing biblical, godly core values will never end. We also understand and know that in times of crisis we will discover the importance of having our values clearly established, or we will find another area to explore our heart and mind with the Word and Spirit of God to add another value to our lives. We also know that, in the seasonal transitions of life, it almost al-ways requires entering the process again. ͵

Core Values Throughout the Seasons of Life

Dick: Over the years, Mary and I have had to recog-nize that, in our season of life as grandparents, it has been required that we seek the Lord about what is important to Him regarding our role and stewardship as "Grandpa and Grandma." As we are blessed with ten grandchildren ranging in years from twenty-two down to age five, we have found this an exciting and enjoyable season of life. Although in our seventies, we are still engaged in full-time ministry which includes international travel each year. Early on, as our grandchildren began arriving, we knew that we needed to seek the Lord as to what would please Him as we moved into this role of our lives.

It wasn't long into this process that one day I sensed the Spirit speaking, "Do not sacrifice your grandchildren at the altar of ministry." Over the years of walking with the Lord, I have learned that the Word of God is true, if you ask for bread, God will not give you a stone (Matthew 7:9 paraphrased)! As Mary and I contemplated what we sensed the Lord was saying, we knew that we needed to put some practical application into this new value.

This has been an amazing experience for Mary and me as we have engaged this grandparenting role. God speak-ing into my spirit not to sacrifice our grandchildren at the altar of ministry really got my attention. As we talked about what the Lord might be saying, it became clear that we wanted to develop a plan or strategy that was prac-tical and doable. So, we started by talking to our three children and their spouses advising them that we wanted to be 'engaged' grandparents by taking an active role in their children's lives. On a practical level that meant that I would adjust my calendar to accommodate special activities and family events in order for us to spend quality time with each of our grandchildren.

First, we decided that we would grandparent together—spending quality time with each of our grandchildren, individually, during their summer vacation from school. Additionally, as each grandchild turned age ten, Mary and I would take them on a special trip (destination of their desire, within reason) and build memories! On top of that, because my ministry calendar gets filled with travel away from home, Mary has a bright green wall marker at her disposal. At any time one of our children calls us with a request to provide care for their children, Mary can go to my office wall calendar to see if there is "white space" for the dates requested. If so, she can use that wonderful little green marker and reserve that time for us to "grandparent together."

Not only have we been able to enjoy our grandchildren during their summer vacations, but I've also enjoyed special events such as taking my oldest grandson to the 2008 Olympic Outreach in China for which he raised his own support. By the time this book goes to press, Mary and I will have taken our oldest granddaughter on a special 'Senior Trip' to California. Our desire and intent is to be engaged not only relationally, but also spiritually in each of their lives, so that their faith in Christ might become personal and a vital part of their daily walks.

Let me recommend two great resources to help you initiate and explore ideas for developing core values in your grandparenting journey. *Extreme Grandparenting* by Dr. Tim & Darcy Kimmel (Focus on the Family) and *Creating a Spiritual Legacy* by Daniel Taylor (Brazos Press).

No matter what season of life we are in, it's important that we develop a core values grid through which we can process the decisions of life that we face daily. So, don't delay; get started today!

The Journey Never Ends

We encourage you to live in the process of discovering and creating healthy, God-intended core values in your life. As you intentionally set out on this journey, it will change everything! Furthermore, the process never ends. There is always a new place to explore as you seek your core, your inner being, and allow the Lord and His Word to bring truth into areas that have been ruled by the stronghold of lies.

CHAPTER FIFTEEN

CREATING CORE VALUES
DIRECTLY FROM SCRIPTURE

The majority of our core values can be taken directly from the Word of God. The Bible is full of God's values that are true and life giving. After an individual becomes redeemed and born again into Jesus Christ, they begin the journey of complete life transformation. Being born again in their spirit and heart, they can then begin the process of renewing their mind.

> I appeal to you therefore, brothers, by the mercies of God, to present your bodies as a living sacrifice, holy and acceptable to God, which is your spiritual worship. Do not be conformed to this world, but be transformed by the renewal of your mind, that by testing you may discern what is the will of God, what is good and acceptable and perfect. (Rom. 12:1-2)

May I suggest that a significant part of this *"renewal"* process is the exchanging of our old-man core beliefs and values for our new-creation core beliefs and values? This thinking identifies with *"by testing you may discern what is the will of God, what is good and acceptable and perfect."* The will of God is *His value*. Unfortunately, most believers don't see the simple, but powerful, reality of this process, and few are intentionally doing anything about it.

Most often, it's the journey of life and external circumstances that thrust us into making critical and life-changing decisions. Even in this, we often don't see the opportunity to become intentional in the process. We need to take time to discover our old, wrong values and seek God's Word and wisdom to establish new, life-giving core values.

The book of Proverbs is made up of the words of a wise man (under the inspiration of God's Spirit) offering life-giving core values to those in need of transformation. There are 31 chapters of core-value statements in this book. The writer is pleading with all of us to ponder these statements and make them our own. He promises that the ones who establish them in their mind and heart will find life.

The Bible reveals God, who He is, and His Core! The Bible is God's gift to each of us to discover Him and all His life-giving truth.

Grady: About ten years into my pastoral ministry, I experienced the powerful benefit of discovering a compelling core value directly from a couple verses in the Bible. It is still amazing to me that one can read a Bible verse over and over and not see its truth. However, the Holy Spirit knows to bring it into focus when we need it. By the way, this happens more often when we are looking for these moments and, of course, are keeping ourselves in the practice of reading the Scripture regularly.

I found myself in a difficult situation as a young pastor. I found myself in contention with a key, influential member of my church. No matter what I did, it seemed this individual was on the other side of the issue or decision. I said red, she said black. After months of this growing frustration, I found that I was becoming bitter toward this individual, and my appreciation for her was lacking and certainly not Christ-like.

When I saw her, I would go the other way! I didn't want

to see her, talk to her, and of course, I didn't have much good to think or say about her. After some time, (too much time) I realized that something was wrong with me, or at least my inability to care for her and be her pastor was in jeopardy. Up to this point of time, I had only focused on her flaws and inappropriate behavior. However, I had finally come to a place of examining my own inability to be Christ-like in this situation. It was time to go to the Word.

What do we do when someone mistreats us, rejects us, sins against us, and creates conflict and problems for us and others? What do we do when someone else is wrong and we are right? Well as I contemplated these questions, I realized that in the flesh (in my old nature) the answer is to reject, correct, and dismiss that person. To build a wall and system of protection from them and do what I can to eliminate their influence in my life.

However, I also knew that all those responses were not Christ-like and not promoted in Scripture. I knew the answer but had not yet come to a place of fully believing in my heart what my mind knew was true. So now I had to search the Scripture once again to find my value and decide if I wanted to make it my own belief.

After some searching, I clearly found my answer. I was reading Ephesians because I knew it was written to a congregation that was struggling to find unity and value with one another as a family of believers. That was where I was. I was struggling to value and love this person that was "sinning against" me. There it was:

"Be kind to one another, tenderhearted, forgiving one another, as God in Christ forgave you." (Eph. 4:32)

And in Colossians:

"Bearing with one another and, if one has a complaint against another,

forgiving each other; as the Lord has forgiven you, so you also must forgive." (Col. 3:13)

It was a core value that was there all the time. Now, would I make it my value? Would I decide to forgive others, even those who have done me wrong, behaved improperly, even hurt me? Or, would I hold on to my old value of protecting myself, punishing the one I thought was wrong, reject them because of their weakness? By the grace of God, I established a new core value in my life at that time. I would "forgive as Christ has <u>forgiven</u> me." Placing my clear belief in that simple biblical statement changed my life and ministry from that day forward and still has such power in my life today. I didn't have to make something up from nothing. It was right there in the Word of God all the time. Many, or even most, of my core value statements that I have established in my life are directly from the words and truth of Scripture.

> *Many of my core value statements… are directly from the words and truth of Scripture.*

We have both had this experience often. As Dick shared earlier, "Owe no man nothing but love," gave him the simple statement of truth and belief he and Mary needed to place its powerful life-changing truth into a core value. That core value would eventually free them from financial bondage and bring them into freedom in Christ.

CHAPTER SIXTEEN

CREATING CORE VALUES WITHIN A
SABBATICAL LIFESTYLE

The journey of developing and living our core values can only be of value and bring life if it is done within the reality and context of having an active, daily relationship with the personal, Triune God. Therefore, this must be one of the foundational core values that our "action values" are built upon. For me, this comes from having a core value to live a sabbatical lifestyle.

A book can be written solely on the topic of Sabbath, so we won't nearly cover that entire topic just now. However, I do want to share briefly what I mean by *living a sabbatical lifestyle*.

Please note, I'm not speaking of an Old Covenant, law-based Sabbath. I'm referring to what I call a "New Covenant" Sabbath that comes from the gift God gave to Adam, and those following, that focuses upon the relational desire God had for Himself and His created sons and daughters. It is simply believing that God wants to have regular and ongoing opportunities for each person to spend relational time with Him and with those we are most closely attached to like our family and community of believers.

I often say, "God is always doing many things at the same time." However, without taking time to listen to God and hear Him, we may only see or focus on one thing. This can be a serious shortcoming when making critical decisions. I believe that all my decisions and actions flow out of my core values (whether consciously or unconsciously). Therefore, I must seek to hear God and discover through His Word and Spirit my significant next moves if I'm to discern correctly and find the peace of God to move forward in His will. I have come to believe and experience the reality that if I am to have core values that are based on truth in Christ, then I must have times of Sabbath rest—times of listening intently to the Word and Spirit of God. This is one of the necessary disciplines to discovering and establishing right core values.

To establish life-giving core values, I must invest time in the process of discernment. This mostly happens in times intentionally devoted to contemplative listening, being quiet, responsive prayer and seeking God's voice. I have discovered there is a definite correlation and marriage of core values, Sabbath, and discernment whereby each allows the other to give life. If I am to discern effectively, I must know what drives my decision making, and this is where I find my core values. The way to find my core values is during intentional times of searching my heart intently. As I take time to search for and discover my core values, my true self and motives are revealed.

Discernment involves the searching of my heart. During the process of searching (which most often takes place in my Sabbath times), God reveals my core to me, my motives or truth of what drives my actions and decisions. Most often, it is at this place God does His greatest work in changing and shaping me back into what He created me to be.

Gordon T. Smith, in his book, *"Listening to God in Times of Choice,"* states it very accurately:

The matter of our motives is of fundamental importance in the task of discernment. We assess our consolation and determine if our peace is from God by reflecting on our motives, specifically: the desire for honor, the desire for wealth, and the desire for security. Each of these can cloud the issues we face and disable in the task of discernment. Effective discernment demands that we know ourselves and are honest with ourselves, particularly when it comes to the values that drive us.

Therefore, it is essential to a mature spirituality and to effective discernment that we test our motives, clarify what values are driving us, especially at the critical junctures of our lives, and turn back to a life that is ordered toward the love of God and His glory. . . A time of decision calls us back to the fundamental choices we have made and the centrality of Christ in our lives." (Gordon T. Smith, *Listening to God in Times of Choice: The Art of Discerning God's Will,* IVP Books, 1997, pp. 63-64)

Sound, biblically based, God-centered core values, will often be discovered and established during the times we need to make critical deci-

> *...God-centered core values will often be established during the times we need to make critical decisions.*

sions. I would venture to say that most people don't intentionally plan or take the time to allow this process of deep relational contemplation to take place in their minds and hearts. So, they keep making poor, life-draining decisions and act in a way that seeks honor and esteem from man. They pursue earthly wealth and provision and self-security instead of trusting in God's love, provision, and true security that comes only from the Father, Son, and Holy Spirit.

I have watched Dick, my mentor and friend, exemplify a daily devotional rhythm that has led him to such a deep relationship that his "core" beliefs and values have developed and been planted deeply within his life. He has maintained a rhythm of relationship with the Lord that has brought such clarity of Christ in his life.

Daily Devotional Rhythm

Scripture verses: Ps 40:1-3, 2Cor 5:17, Luke 7:47, John 15, Ps 1:1-3

The following scriptures help us to see how both the Lord Jesus and King David modeled and exhibited the importance and intimacy of having time alone with God!

And rising very early in the morning, while it was still dark, He departed and went out to a desolate place, and there He prayed. (Mark 1:35)

As a deer pants for flowing streams, so pants my soul for You, O God, My soul thirsts for God, for the living God. (Ps. 42:1-2)

Dick: After more than forty years of walking with my Lord Jesus Christ, experiencing the ongoing revelation of my Father's unconditional love, and the fellowship of the Holy Spirit, I find it a healthy exercise to reflect on my daily devotional rhythm. As you might imagine, there have been many peaks and valleys over the past four decades, but I cannot recall one time where I've felt abandoned by the Lord. As I write this, Mary and I are on vacation in the mountains of Colorado, and in our daily drives, we are experiencing the reality of many natural peaks and valleys making it easy to reflect on my journey.

Since that Sunday morning back in January of 1976, I've always had a deep hunger and love for the Word of God! Additionally, since I'm a morning person, it's been only natural for me to rise early and spend time alone with the Lord. As mentioned earlier, because I've encountered that still small voice speaking to me through the Scriptures and in the quietness of my times of worship,

I have great anticipation that the Lord is always ready to meet with me.

Early in my faith walk, one Scripture that had a huge impact on me is:

> *"He also brought me up out of a horrible pit, out of the miry clay, and set my feet upon a rock, and established my steps. He has put a new song in my mouth, Praise to our God; Many will see and fear, and will trust in the Lord." (Ps. 40:2-3, NKJV)*

I witnessed the reality of these verses very early in my faith in Christ. Within two years of my coming to Christ, over twenty-five members of my family and extended family professed faith in Christ. The Lord allowed me to walk in a deep revelation of the depravity of my soul and wretchedness of my sin while at the same time revealing His grace and unending love for me. Somehow, I knew that I had been forgiven so much and was loved so much that I wanted to pour out my love back to God:

> *"Therefore I say to you, her sins, which are many, are forgiven, for she loved much. But to whom little is forgiven, the same loves little." (Luke 7:47, NKJV)*

My soul was so hungry for His Presence that I would spend the early morning hours in worship, study of the Word, and in prayer with thanksgiving and praise unto Jesus. My soul thirsted for the living God (Ps 42:2)!

During those early years of my faith, I was still in the corporate world traveling each week from Kansas City to numerous other cities in the Midwest and beyond at times. I knew very little about the tithe at that time, yet unending hunger inside of me caused me to rise early giving the Lord the "first fruits" of each day.

As I was being discipled, I began to memorize and meditate on these verses in Psalms:

Blessed is the man who walks not in the counsel of the wicked, nor stands in the way of sinners, nor sits in the seat of scoffers; but his delight is in the law of the Lord, and on his law he meditates day and night. He is like a tree planted by streams of water that yields its fruit in its season, and its leaf does not wither. In all that he does, he prospers. (Psalm 1:1-3)

These verses and John 15:1-5 became the anchor for my daily devotionals. That soon expanded to reading five Psalms each day (based on the calendar date) plus the Proverb of day. There, of course, were times when this pattern was broken, but it wouldn't be long before I found myself returning to it to find comfort, wisdom, and direction for my daily life.

I have many friends (well, I believe they are still friends) who have traveled to China and other countries with me over these past twenty years that have experienced my early morning devotional rhythm and coffee brewing around 4:30 or 5 a.m.

I certainly realize that not everyone is a morning person and perhaps that is not your best time to meet with God. However, I discovered early in my journey that I "leak" and that I must have that daily communion with my Lord to face whatever the day might hold for me. Let me encourage you to find the daily devotional rhythm that best suits you! It's much better than any American Express card—you don't want to leave home without having met with the Master!

It is in this journey of being in the Scriptures through a daily devotional rhythm that my mind is continually being renewed. The Holy Spirit puts His finger on those areas of my life that have yet to be fully sanctified (1 Thess. 5:23). The Living Word of God—the Lord Jesus Christ—is the "plumb line" to which I am being conformed daily by His kindness, mercy, and grace!

What we are proposing is the simple reality and need we each have to spend time with the Lord allowing us to listen to His voice. In these times, He will reveal our true heart of faith and belief and help us see our true core values versus His core values. This is when we receive revelation of belief (or lack thereof) in His life-giving truth. Discovering and establishing biblical core values is not merely an academic exercise or discipline. It often is only fully discovered and realized through times of devotional relationship with God.

CHAPTER SEVENTEEN

CORE VALUES AND VOWS

Grady: As we go through life, from childhood and adolescence into early adulthood and beyond, we establish core values (often unknowingly) that direct our every decision and action. When we establish and form a core value based upon a lie (or based upon something other than God's truth), it may have come from a vow made in our lives. A vow is more than a casual belief; it intentionally gives emotional and spiritual ground to the lie.

Let me share an example of a vow from my own life. When I was about eight years old, I had a bed-wetting problem. This was something I never recalled in my consciousness. During my sabbatical retreat, when I had asked God for what I should deal with in my heart for the next year, remember He had given me the word "humiliation." I had no idea how this word related to a heart issue in my life at that time, but that was about to change over the next few hours and days.

As I asked the Lord about this word, He began to stir up my memory. I saw myself when I was about eight sitting in the corner of our old house. I had a pair of underwear around my neck—wet underwear. My dad apparently thought this would be the cure to my bed-wetting problem. With this picture vividly in my awareness, the Lord spoke to me very clearly. He said, "When you were sitting in that chair, you said in your heart that you would never allow anyone to humiliate you again." That was a vow. At that moment, my life would forever be affected by my establishing this core value in my mind and heart.

Over the next several months, during times of contemplation and prayer, the Lord continued to reveal the impact brought on by the core value established by that vow in my heart. As I began to journey into my past, the Holy Spirit began to bring back specific remembrance of the affects this vow had upon many actions and decisions I had made in my life.

I began to see why I had struggled so much with certain fears in my life's journey. I was afraid to speak in public (isn't everyone?), I was easily embarrassed for myself and even others, I avoided many opportunities because of a fear something would go wrong and I would look foolish. I struggled to receive compliments, thanks, or any kind of praise for my efforts. It had a powerful influence over me becoming an unhealthy perfectionist. Nothing I did could measure up to my own impossible demand of perfection. So, often I would quit operating in the gifts God had placed in my possession because I was afraid of the possibility of being humiliated. However, I hadn't even known what was at the core of this mess.

Nothing I did could measure up to my own impossible demand of perfection.

That wasn't even the worst of it! As I explored this stronghold and core value, the Lord revealed more truth and painful reality. He showed me that I had become so entangled and familiar with the fear of humiliation that I had learned how to use it as a weapon toward others. I knew the power of humiliation and knew how to spew it on others to manipulate, control, or hurt them. This was the most difficult part of the journey for me. The enemy had not only taken away from my own life because of this core value, but he had used this lie through me to hurt others. As the Lord began to reveal, heal, and reestablish new belief and truth in my mind and heart regarding the issue of humiliation, He continued to reveal its far-reaching impact and effect in other relationships in my life.

One example was my relationship with my mother. It was about 2005, when I had an important conversation with Dick regarding an issue I had with my mom. I explained to him that often, when I was with my mother (she had been living in our home since 1997), I would find myself feeling anger toward her. I explained how bizarre this was because I had no logical explanation for this anger. My mom had done nothing but love and care for me all my life. I was clueless where this feeling of anger had come from. Dick agreed to pray for me that the Lord would reveal the root of this anger.

It was several years later, while on this journey of dealing with the stronghold of humiliation, that the Lord revealed the reason for my anger toward my mother. I recall the moment vividly when it all became clear. I was with Dick in New York leading a retreat for a group of church leaders. During one of our breaks, I took a walk into the woods and sat by a beautiful spring of running water. It was a great opportunity to hear from the Lord and continue to delve into the humiliation issue.

Once again, I asked the Holy Spirit to reveal more to me regarding what needed to be understood if I were to gain complete freedom from this stronghold. At that moment, He answered Dick's and my prayers regarding the anger with my mother. The Spirit spoke clearly to me. "Grady, the reason you experience anger toward your mother is that she isn't afraid of humiliation." It all began to come into focus for me.

My mom had more than her share of hurt. My grandparents had divorced when my mother was fourteen. She married at eighteen and had a struggling marriage that ended in tragedy. She gave up her four children to adoption believing (and being told by family) it was the best thing for them. Her marriage with *my* birth father ended quickly after my birth, and life was hard for her.

In all this pain, she never became bitter, unforgiving, or self-protective. Growing up I never heard her whine, complain, or reveal any self-pity. She rarely spoke unkindly about or toward anyone, not even those who had hurt her and had used or treated her poorly. My mom was the kindest person I have ever known, and I was angry about it!

Why was this? Because in my incorrect thinking, she allowed people to humiliate her, treat her disrespectfully, and take advantage of her kindness. For me, living with a vow and core value that I would never let anyone humiliate me, I couldn't deal with her freedom from my lie.

At that moment, for the first time, my anger for my mom was covered by God's atonement. I asked the Lord to forgive me and prayed again that I would be free from any power from that vow I had made so long ago. I wanted to be free from the fear of humiliation like my mom.

Furthermore, it not only affected me in the realm of humiliation, but through that vow, I also gave the enemy a foothold to allow anger for my stepfather.

Therefore, having put away falsehood, let each one of you speak the truth with his neighbor, for we are members one of another. Be angry and do not sin; do not let the sun go down on your anger, and give no opportunity to the devil. (Eph. 4:25-27)

In this one experience, I naively created a belief and, unknowingly, established a core value upon a lie that would allow one of those strongholds in my heart and mind such as those that are mentioned in 2 Corinthians 10:4. This stronghold affected many areas of my life for many years.

I continue to be set free from the stronghold of humiliation. The core value I now am learning to believe and live by is that "I am willing to be a fool for Christ."

Dick: The great commandments: "Love God, Love Others" are all about living in relationship with the One who created us in His image so that we might enjoy fellowship with Him and our fellow human beings.

As a boy growing up, our family moved a lot, and I attended at least ten different schools from kindergarten through high school, always finding myself in search of new friends. One of the qualities that I inherited from my father was that he had "never met a stranger," so it seemed only natural for me to find new friends and develop a relationship with them no matter where I found myself.

Early in my journey with the Lord Jesus Christ, the Holy Spirit began to reveal to me, or should I say convict my heart, about unhealthy dynamics that existed within my own family. One of those relationships was with my father. As stated briefly in an earlier chapter, our family was quite dysfunctional considering my father's alcoholism and related issues that existed within our family system. This, of course, is not surprising when you consider that my dad ran away from home at age fifteen carrying many wounds and deep anger in his heart. Then he married my mother at age eighteen. He knew nothing except to work and to fight for everything that he was going to get in life.

I certainly received some of my work ethic from my hard-working dad. Following in his footsteps, I was working fifty-five plus hours a week in the insurance business while at the same time pastoring a new church plant on weekends. As a result, in May of 1980, I found myself flat on my back suffering from mono.

Little did I realize that the Lord was about to break into a very closed-off area of my heart that would transform the way I would see and do relationships for the rest of my life. He would reveal to me the importance of being intentional and obedient not only to the Word of God, but also to live with a great sensitivity to the leading of His Holy Spirit!

On that beautiful, spring day, while lying there in the quiet on my sickbed, I heard a still, small voice say "Son, you have a competitive spirit toward your father."

I was alarmed at what I had just heard and responded immediately to this inner voice as if to defend myself, "What do You mean, Lord? I love my dad!" My father had come to Christ two years after I had in 1978, and the Lord had delivered him from alcohol and was doing an amazing work in his life.

Instantly, I heard in my spirit, "I know you love him, but that's not what I want to talk to you about." Suddenly, I found myself caught up in this dialog with the Lord and engulfed in an overwhelming sense of peace. I asked the Lord what He meant by a "competitive spirit," and almost immediately, I had a very vivid memory of myself when I was about nine years old.

As a young boy, I would spend time every summer with my mother's parents in a small town in northwest Iowa. Grandpa and Grandma owned a grocery store there, and I always looked forward to staying with them each summer as I loved working in the store, stocking shelves, and grinding the ground beef as well as sacking and carrying out groceries for the customers—always talking and meeting new friends.

I saw myself walking into the pool hall located in the little town where they had their grocery store. My buddies and I had been out playing baseball and working up a sweat on that hot summer day. The only cool place in town was the local bar, so we were taking a break and going to play a little pool. As I was passing by the bar, an old man looked at me and called me up to him saying, "Are you Sally Dungan's boy?" (My dad's name was Sylvester, but his nickname was Sally.)

I saw myself responding rather proudly with an immediate, "Yes sir!"

Without hesitation, the old man said, "Do you think you'll ever be half the man your ole man is?" And, with that, I saw myself shrink back, not saying a word and walk away.

I was stunned by what I had just seen, and I responded by asking the Lord to help me understand what He was showing me. My dialog with the Lord continued for some time as I lay there on my sickbed. The Holy Spirit revealed to me how the words of that old man had been operating as a curse in my life since the day they were spoken over me. My response to his words had been inward where I had made a vow in my heart saying, "I'm going to be better than my ole man, even if it kills me!" Those words had become a driving force in my life, and there is not enough room in this book to relate all the times in my life that it nearly killed me.

Over the next couple of hours, the Holy Spirit showed me that I needed to repent of my anger toward that old man, to forgive him, and release him into the Lord's hands. I needed to renounce that inner vow that I had made, breaking the power of that "competitive spirit" toward my father, blessing, and releasing my father into the Lord's hands as well. I was then prompted by the Holy Spirit to write my father a letter expressing gratitude for all the good things that he had deposited into my life. This took several days as the process brought up some very painful childhood memories for which I, over and over, had to forgive, release, and bless my father. By the time I mailed that letter, I was totally free of any anger, bitterness, or competitiveness toward my father. Sixteen years later, after preaching at my father's funeral in 1996, my mother gave me Dad's Bible, and I found that letter, for which I had never received an acknowledgment, tucked behind the inside cover. Mom later told me that my father would begin his quiet time on many occasions by opening, reading, and then replacing my letter inside the cover of his Bible.

This began an amazing journey in which I would begin to understand the importance of recognizing inner vows. It also helped me realize the power they had in establishing core values which allowed the enemy to establish strongholds. These strongholds created some significant, unhealthy thinking and behavior with relationships with my father (and others). It also taught me to be intentional in obedience to the leading of the Holy Spirit when it comes to restoring relationships.

I didn't know I had a core value that I needed to compete with my father or realize the impact that belief had on my relationship with my father and others. Now that I saw this clearly, renounced it, forgave him, and repented, I could establish a new core value and belief that "I am not in competition with my father or others."

The Reward of Becoming Free From Improper Vows & Unhealthy Core Values:

Dick Continues: In October of '93, I was preparing to facilitate the travel of seventy-five pastors and church leaders to do church planting in Russia. It was during this time that I kept hearing that still small voice saying, "I want you to go to your father and ask him for a father's blessing." I hadn't read Gary Smalley and John Trent's book, *The Blessing*, at that time, and so, busy with preparation and not really understanding what the prompting was all about, I just kept putting it off. Finally, one morning just a couple days before departure, I was sitting at my desk, and I heard a rather strong prompting, "Are you going to obey me or not?"

Without hesitation I responded, "What do you mean, Lord?"

His response was immediate, "I told you to go to your father and ask him to pray a Father's Blessing over you!"

I replied with something like "I don't even know what that is, Lord."

To which I heard the following "Trust Me, and I'll lead you."

With that I picked up the phone and called my father who lived a couple hours away and said, "Hey Dad, are you and Mom going to be home? I want to run over to see you before I leave for Russia."

"Is everything alright?"

I assured him, "Everything's fine; just want to see you before I take off. I'll be over in a couple hours. Have the coffee pot on," and hung up. Sure enough, I could smell the fresh coffee brewing as I walked through the door of that old farm house. At this point, I was thinking more about just being obedient rather than having any clue as to what the Lord was up to. As I sat down and Mom poured me a fresh cup of brew, I began in my attempt to explain why it was important for me to interrupt my busy morning with a four-hour drive (round trip) to say good-bye before leaving for Russia. I finally said to my father, "The Lord told me to come over and have you give me a father's blessing."

When he promptly asked what that was, I shared my limited understanding with something like "Well, just stand over me, lay hands on me, and tell the Lord whatever comes to your mind."

Mom chimed in quickly with, "Can I do it too?"

I assured her that it would be great if she wanted to as both got up and stood over me putting their hands on my shoulders. Dad led out with "Well, Lord, I sure am proud of my son, and it sure would be nice if You would bring him back safe from Russia." He said a couple more things, said "Amen," and then waited for Mom to pray. Honestly, I wish I could remember what my mother said, but I was so caught up in my father's words which I had never heard before that nothing else registered. They sat back down and we visited a little more, and it was soon time for me to leave.

Then something very profound happened! As I got up to hug and kiss them goodbye, I kept hearing "Fulfill, fulfill, fulfill..." in my spirit. As I walked to the doorway leading out to the porch, these words kept getting stronger and stronger.

Upon reaching the doorway, I turned around and there was my father standing just inches away from me, face to face! Out of my mouth came the following words as I looked into my father's eyes, "The Lord would have you to know that He is going to fulfill through my life what has always been in your heart." Immediately, my father fell into my arms weeping as I held him for what seemed like several minutes. It is so amazing what God wants to do if we will just be obedient and intentional!

As Paul Harvey would say, "And now, for the rest of the story." I mentioned earlier, my father ran away from home at age fifteen and always had a soft spot in his heart for the broken, hurting, and beaten down young people in life.

Even prior to becoming Christians, Dad and Mom were always helping those who were down and out, the orphan or homeless, most of which took advantage of them. They lied and stole from them showing very little appreciation for what my parents had done for them. Now, fast forward to 2010 and I'm in Hong Kong with my dear friend and ministry board member, Bob Fulling, ministering to several orphan teenagers who have been taken in off the street, led to Christ, and discipled by a precious Chinese woman who was given the English name Candy. For two days, I'd been teaching on the power of forgiveness, and at the beginning of the third day, it became apparent that the Holy Spirit was speaking to the hearts of these precious young Chinese orphans. It became obvious that it was time to lead them through the process of forgiving so that healing could be released into each of their hearts. As I stood over one of the young men praying for him, he began to sob, and tears flowed down his cheeks. I saw a vision of an open heaven with my father standing and looking down upon what was happening, a huge smile on his face, his hand outstretched toward me, and saying "Way to go son, I'm so proud of you!"

Hebrews says:

Therefore we also, since we are surrounded by so great a cloud of witnesses... (Heb. 12:1 NKJV).

If you choose to enter the process, be aware that the Lord may have much to reveal to you about vows and strongholds in your own life. As you become aware of these realities, it is important to seek forgiveness, give forgiveness, and be set free from these strongholds. However, it is also critical to not stop there. This is one of the main reasons we focus so much on core values. The vow, the lie, and any stronghold must be replaced with truth! If not, the lie can easily return and take root in old familiar ground.

SECTION FIVE:

Engaging the Process

CHAPTER EIGHTEEN

HOW TO GET STARTED

Identify Your Current Core Values

The best way we have found to begin the process is to block out some time to be alone so that you can clear your mind from distractions. Ideally, take at least a 24-hour retreat away from your busy life. Find a place you can get quiet. This will allow you to explore and hear the things deep inside your mind and heart. However, if you can't get away, just take a few hours, or an hour a day for a week to begin the process.

Prayer

To begin, take some time to pray and invite the Holy Spirit to lead you into your journey of identifying your core values. This is very important to the process. We have found that our heavenly Father is waiting for this prayer. He wants to lead us on the journey of exploring and discovering our core beliefs about Him, ourselves, and others. Prayer invites God into your journey, and He will speak to you along the way.

Choose an Area to Explore

Next, choose the area you want to explore. If you want to go for the foundational/internal core values, we recommend choosing an area of relationship. I always suggest starting with the realm of "self"! Ask the question, "What do I believe about who I am?" This is the most significant area of your life and affects all the other areas of your life. A worksheet to help you get started can be found in Appendix C.

If you want to begin more simply, just choose a topic to explore. (See Appendix B for an example.) For example, what are your core values regarding money or ministry? This is usually easier because it seems more tangible than relationships. However, the goal will be to find the foundational core value even though you will begin looking at how you behave and act with your topic.

Grady: Remember my example of why I tithe? My behavior was to tithe based on the foundational core value that God commanded and gave me an obligation to give a tithe. However, as I explored this area of my life, I realized that my foundational core value was flawed. As I explored the Scriptures, I realized that I needed to create a new core value that the tithe should be given because I believe God is the provider of all my needs and loves me. Therefore, I now tithe as an act of faith in this new reality, and I give cheerfully because I am thankful. It is no longer an obligation.

A Journey into the Past

Again, the search for your established core values is a journey of discovery and exploration. You will be surprised what you will find as you contemplate the different aspects and levels of where your core values and beliefs have come from in your life.

It is a healthy adventure. However, quite often, as you take this journey, you will discover or reconnect with realities that will touch upon deep emotions, good and bad.

As mentioned earlier, you may discover unhealthy "vows" and "promises" you have made that keep you stuck in a harmful core value. Don't be afraid of this possibility, it is part of the value of the journey. It creates opportunity for further spiritual, intellectual, and emotional formation or reformation that will lead to further growth and revelation of who you are in Christ! It will help you clarify what values you already have that are healthy and biblically sound. Furthermore, it will also allow you to discover the values that are not healthy or God-inspired. That is the life-giving reward for such an intentional voyage.

Ask the Questions

Begin to ask the who, what, and why questions. There is more than one way to do this. Again, we believe that the Holy Spirit can lead you to the questions. If you're exploring what you believe about "self," then ask, "Who am I? Who does God say I am? Who do other people say I am?" If it's something like money, ask, "What do I think about money? What did my family system teach me about money? How did my parents handle money?" As you ask the questions, answers will begin to flow. Write down the answers. Often it is best to go back to the early years of your life. Often, creating a timeline with your journey into the past can be helpful and revealing (especially in relationships).

Grady: When I wanted to find my core value about tithing, my first question was, "When did I first hear about tithing?" I recalled a conversation I had with my pastor when I was 16 years old. He explained some of the commands of God and the concept that it was an issue of obedience. That established the foundational core value for me at that time and remained the reason for my tithing for the next 14 years of my life. However, when I was 30 years old, I asked another question, "What does the Bible really say about tithing?" It was then that I discovered some new information that would lead me to establish a new core value that changed my reason for giving a tithe.

Questions are a key part of the process. This takes time as you explore your past, and one question and its answer will almost always lead to other questions. Eventually, it will lead you to your foundational core values that already exist. This is the goal. When you discover the core belief, you can then move on to the next step in the process. Don't be in a rush to get through this step. Remember, this is a relational process as well as an intellectual exercise.

What Does the Bible Reveal?

When I began to clearly discover my core value of self, it became clear that some things were unhealthy and untrue. I realized that I thought of myself as an orphan, full of fear, imperfect, inadequate, and never good enough! I found many of the reasons for this wrong thinking and for the flawed core values I had established from this wrong thinking and belief foundation. Now, I had to go on a journey with God and His Word. It took several years to reshape and rebuild my core value of self. The Word of God was revealing the truth to me, and I could identify the truth in which I began to place my faith. My life began to change significantly.

At this stage of the process, as you pray, you are asking God and searching in His Word for answers to the questions you have already asked yourself. OK, God, I need to know what you say about who I am or about the reason to tithe. As you read the Bible, His Word begins to reveal the answer. When you find Scriptures and statements that speak to the core value you are exploring, write them down. A concordance and other Bible study tools will help in this stage of the process.

One of the things I believed about myself was: "I can't do anything well enough. Many times throughout my life, I would not take certain risks for fear of failure or falling short. This allowed the enemy to discourage me, keeping me from life-giving obedience and hindering my joy. As I began to explore Scripture, I discovered that although I can't do anything perfectly (no one can), the Word says in Philippians 4:13 that: *"I can do all things through Christ who strengthens me."* Romans 8:31 states, *"...If God is for us who can be against us?"* What is the truth? The greater truth is that I can do whatever I feel God asks me to do (even though on my own, I may fail) because I can trust Him and believe He can do any work through me! I began to see myself differently.

In most cases, you can find God's truth for all the areas you seek. When you know what you already believed and see what God's Word and Spirit reveal as true, you can choose where to place your faith. Now you can establish healthy core values, and your decisions and actions will lead you to life and not defeat.

Define Your Core Value

As you continue this journey of finding and establishing life-giving core values, your life will change. Your mind will begin to be renewed, and you will begin to learn to live as a "new creature." Your identity will become what God says, not what this fallen world calls you. How you see and use money will change! Your ministry will become less of a burden and more fruitful and fulfilling. Change whatever area you delve into, and life will come as you practice this process.

Write down what you discovered to be God's values.

> *As you continue this journey of finding and establishing life-giving core values, your life will change.*

Here is an example of what I discovered and am now placing my faith in about myself:

- I was created to be a son of God, my loving Creator.
  He is my Father who provides for me and protects
  me in all things!
- My value and worth come from the reality that God
  loves me fully because I am His son. I know that I
  am His son because I have surrendered myself to
  His love and redemption through His Son, the Lord
  Jesus Christ.
- I have a calling and mission within the kingdom of
  God on this earth. I have been given the opportu-
  nity to be a vessel of honor that God can pour into
  and out of in this life He has given me.

As I revisit the different areas of my core values over
the years, I continue to discover and add more truth to
my list. The process has now become a normal and active
part of my daily life. I live in the process and continually
find more life.

Make a Commitment to Your Core Values

This is where everything you have done in the process
comes to life and changes you forever. As you write out
your new core values, you must place your faith in God
and what He has revealed to you in your mind and heart.
Knowledge gives you an opportunity to change, but faith
in your heart (belief) is what makes it alive and real.

We must begin to walk in the core values we have
clearly established in our minds and act upon what we
now believe is true. When Peter determined to walk to
Jesus on the water, he had to believe that when Jesus
said come, he could come. However, what made it possible, ultimately, were his steps of faith. He had to step to

the edge, lift his legs over, and step on the water before the reality of walking on water could be experienced. However, in this case, Peter's faith didn't last too long as he found himself shifting from his focused belief in what Jesus had stated to the circumstances around him. When he stopped believing, he failed. His core value was still in flux at this point.

If I want my tithe to be a cheerful exercise of giving instead of an obligation, I must choose in my heart to believe that God is my provider, and all I have is a gift from Him. Therefore, when I place that check in the offering box, I now do it believing what I know, that it is about His care and provision for my life and not my act of obedience. So now, with this new core value, I give a tithe with joyful and faithful belief in Him.

Live Your Core Values

As you go through the process of discovering and establishing life-giving core values in your life, you will have to practice them. In this case, practice makes faith. As you step out more and more in what you now have clarified as true, you will begin to experience life. Often, you will take several steps forward and a few back. It is a walk of growing faith. The enemy will wait for opportunities to ambush you and push you back to the old ways—the old core values of your past.

This is not a mathematical equation, it's a journey—it's life. Just keep stepping out in faith in what you discover is true. Peter didn't walk on water long. However, over time he learned to live a life of faith and became what God created him to be and do!

Do It in Community

The process of discovering and establishing is primarily

a personal journey. However, it can also be done in community. Walking through this process with another person such as a spouse, friend, mentor or coach adds a powerful dynamic that can deepen the experience and accelerate the process. This is especially true at the beginning of the journey.

NOTE: See Appendix E for suggestions for processing core values in a small group.

Grady: For me, the first 15 years were primarily a personal experience with some interaction with Sandy. However, since Dick and I discovered we were both on a similar journey, and we became intentional in pursuing the process more, we have taken many opportunities to work on it together. We also have presented it primarily in retreat settings for men and couples. We have found this to be a great way to encourage men and women to engage in the process. You may want to enter this adventure with your spouse or a friend or invite someone to mentor or coach you through the process.

Even if you choose to do most of the processing alone, we suggest you engage with another individual or small group, occasionally, and share your journey with them to help you be accountable. In this way, they can add an outside perspective to strengthen the core values you are establishing in your life. Refinement always needs some outside pressure which forces us to grow and change and this process has a valuable impact upon achieving the highest level of growth. Furthermore, it's just more enjoyable than to go it alone all the time!

In 2006, we began an annual men's retreat that is one of the main ministries we offer to present core values and help men enter the intentional journey and process of discovering and establishing them in their everyday lives.

Explore the possibilities of joining others in the journey of establishing core values.

It's Really the Journey of Discipleship

We are all called to follow Christ and be His disciples! As we learn to follow, He reveals and leads us on the path of becoming all He created us to be. He leads us into the beliefs and faith that will bring us life in Christ. We really want you to understand that it is so much more than a formula or exercise. It is a life-long relational journey with the Triune God: Father, Son, and Holy Spirit. God leads us, and we hear His voice throughout the journey. However, it also must be intentional on our part. We must invite the Lord into the process and see it as an opportunity to spend time with Him. This was part of the great surprise for us. As we engaged in the process, we discovered His presence with us more and more.

CHAPTER NINETEEN

A FINAL WORD

Please consider taking the journey. We believe if you will engage in the process, you will discover the depths of what is already in your heart and be enabled to create clear, life-giving core values that will guide you toward a greater experience of living in the reality of being the son or daughter God created you to be. It's a journey of discovering the new creation you are in Christ.

> *Do not be conformed to this world, but be transformed by the renewal of your mind, that by testing you may discern what is the will of God, what is good and acceptable and perfect. (Rom. 12:2)*

How do we test what we know and believe in our mind? How do we really renew the old values and beliefs of our "old man"? What we have experienced is something we must intentionally engage our focus upon with help from God's Word and Holy Spirit. It is our personal experience and our hope for you that if you choose to engage in this process, you will experience the renewing of your mind. And, in turn, you will believe and establish the values that our Father created you to possess. You will grow in a life-giving faith and belief that is powerful. Furthermore, it will help you be more consistent in making better, life-giving decisions in everyday life as well as in times of crisis and transition.

This process is an exercise of *"testing"* what you believe so that you can end up with a clear knowledge and understanding of the "will of God." Our hope is that you will come to a place of knowing what you believe and create core value statements that will help you place your trust and faith in what is true. This will allow you greater power to choose the truths that will bring a more "acceptable and perfect" life in Christ.

THE PROCESS OF DEVELOPING CORE VALUES

Identify Current Core Values	Identify & Establish Biblical Core Values	Repentance, Forgiveness, & Thanksgiving	Commitment to Biblical CV
Often requires journey into the past process	Seek biblical values through clear value mandates & implied in biblical illustrations	2 Cor. 10:5	Commit to the ongoing refinement

We have tried to keep the process as simple as possible. If you follow the arrow down you see that to identify your current core values, you must intentionally explore what core values you have already established in your mind and heart. This takes prayer, careful thought, and listening to what the Spirit of God reveals and reminds you of regarding the topic or relationship you are exploring. After discovering your current core values, you then move to the next step.

Go to the Scripture with the value you currently hold to be true and compare it to the principles and Spirit of the Word. If they are the same, then write it out and establish it clearly in your mind and spirit so that you are more consciously aware of the value from this day forward. This is very powerful.

However, if your current core value is different or in opposition to what the Bible reveals, then you need to go to step three. Renounce the wrong value, repent, and thank God for the revelation of a better belief and value. Again, write down the new core value, and ask the Lord to help you to clearly establish it in your mind and heart.

Here you may note the arrows point to the biblical reference of II Corinthians 10:5.

When we have an established core value that is contrary to what Scripture indicates as truth, and we want to make the exchange from the *"argument and every lofty opinion raised against the knowledge of God,"* to *"take every thought captive to obey Christ."* This is critical in the process. This is an intellectual exchange, but more importantly, it is a spiritual exchange of faith and belief! This allows the exchange to take place in our whole being. Now, the possibility for a life change is probable.

After this point in the process, it is now simply a matter of clarifying, clearly stating, and intentionally acting upon our value when circumstances arise. When a crisis or situation requiring a decision enters our life, we can make our choices based on what we have clearly established in our mind and heart as biblical, life-giving truth. Victory is now more possible then before.

It is at this final stage of the process, we discover if we have only truthful knowledge or if we also have faith to act upon the truth. Therefore, it is not a seeking of truth alone that frees us, but it is now placing faith in what Christ has revealed to us through His Word and Spirit that brings the real change.

Here is a process outline that can help you work through a topical core value process experience. In this example, the topic is "ministry."

Process Outline/Worksheet:

I. Core Values: In Ministry (Within and Without the Church)

  A. Process: Identify Present Core Values

    1. Our values and beliefs regarding ministry have developed primarily from:

      a. Family system

      b. Early church (or non-church) experience
* Denominational distinctive
* Key pastoral/church leaders

      c. Personal experiences

      d. Cultural influence

      e. Peers

      f. Media

      g. Regional distinctive

      h. Educational influence

      i. Other

    2. Our journey into the past

      a. Questions to consider:
* What was your family's experience and belief about church and ministry?
  - Ministry
  - Ministers
  - Value and function of the church

- What were your early church experiences (ages 0-21)?

b. What were the distinctive Christian practices of your church world?

c. Who were the people you saw as ministers and leaders within the church or ministry part of your life? How did they influence the way you think about ministry and ministers?

d. What are some of the positive and negative experiences you had in the church world you were raised in? If not raised in church, what were your experiences with any type of religious influence?

e. How did the culture influence your concept of ministry?
- Peers
- Media
- Education
- Regional influences, etc.

B. Process: Identify and Establish Biblical Core Values

1. Identify Biblical Core Values

Direct mandates and biblical illustrations
- Almost all the biblical characters (positive and negative)
- Matthew 28:19-20
- Titus
- 1 and 2 Timothy
- 1 Corinthians 12-14
- 2 Corinthians 6
- Romans 7
- Joshua 1

- Proverbs (throughout the entire book)
2. What are other Scriptures that apply to ministry?
3. Distinguish different elements of the Minister
   - Calling/your calling?
   - Gifting/your gifting?
   - Heart/your heart?
   - Character/your character and values?
4. Who and what is a minister?
5. What is ministry?
6. Where and when does ministry take place?
7. What are other experiences, people, or things that have shaped your ideas about doing ministry?
8. Compare old core values with discovered core values through this process and write out new or clarified core values you want to place your faith in for the future.

C. Process: Repentance, Forgiveness and Thanksgiving (if Needed)

1. Journeying into the past can stir up negative experiences, wounds, and mistakes (and positive, thankful feelings)
   a. Need to identify deceptions of belief (strongholds of wrong core values)
      2 Corinthians 10:3-6
   b. Need to identify our duplication, reaction, or differentiation
   c. Need for repentance (release from past mistakes and errors)

    d. Need to forgive (release from blame and judgment) Colossians 3:13 and Ephesians 4:31-32

    e. Need to express gratefulness and thankfulness (Freedom from whatever past experiences and deceptions have had their power in our lives)

2. As a final step, confirm again and write out new or clarified core values you want to place your faith in for the future.

D. Process: Implement and Practice Established Core Values and Fine Tune

Spend some time in prayer committing your mind and heart to the core value the Lord and His Scripture have led you to clearly establish. Ask for grace and faith to live in the core value you have now committed to. As you begin and continue to practice and apply your core values to behavior and decisions, continue to fine-tune your belief statements more precisely and clearly.

This is an example process outline/worksheet that can help you progress through a relational core value. This example is focusing on the core value of "self."

Core Values: In Self

A. Process: Identify Present Core Values

    1. Identify current core values: Journey into the past
- Our values and beliefs regarding our "self" have developed primarily from:
  - The Curse (Genesis 3) "you can be like God" and
  - A separated "orphan" mentality
- Family system
- Early church (or non-church) experience
  - Denominational distinctive
  - Key pastoral/church leaders
- Personal experiences
- Cultural influence peers
- Media
- Regional distinctive
- Educational influence
- Other

    2. Spend time in all the above areas and write down what you know and believe from each of these areas to help you find what you already believe about yourself. Now proceed to the next step.

B. Process: Identify and Establish Biblical Core Values

    1. Identify Biblical Core Values, Direct mandates, and Biblical illustrations regarding self in relationship with God Created in the Godhead's image (Genesis 1:26)

- I am wonderfully made (Psalm 139:14)
- Heirs of God (tripartite promise: "I will be your God, you will be My people, and I will dwell with you." Genesis 12-Revelation 21:3; Romans 4:13; and 1 Peter 1:3-4; Romans 8:17)
- 1 Peter 2:9 (royal priesthood, holy nation,)
- God loves us fully and has proven it (John 3:16)
- I am a new creation (2 Corinthians 5:17)
- We are God's children and His sons (John 1:12, 1 John 4:1-6, Romans 8:14-15)
- I am blessed (Deuteronomy 28:1-6)
- I am a citizen of Heaven (Philippians 3:20, Psalm 15)
- Nothing can separate us from God's love (Romans 8:35-39)
- I am a friend of God (John 15:15)

2. What else does the Bible reveal to us about who we are in Christ?

C. Process: Repentance, Forgiveness, and Thanksgiving (if needed)

1. Compare old core values with newly discovered core values through this process and write out new or clarified core values you want to place your faith in for the future.

2. Journeying into the past can stir up negative experiences, wounds, and mistakes and/or positive, thankful feelings.

- Need to identify deceptions of belief (strongholds of wrong core values) 2 Corinthians 10:3-6
- Need to identify our duplication, reaction, or differentiation
- Need for repentance (release from past mistakes and errors)

- Need to forgive (release from blame and judgment) Colossians 3:13 and Ephesians 4:31,32
- Need to express gratefulness & thankfulness (freedom from whatever past experiences and deceptions have had their power in our lives)

D. Process: Commit to Your Established Core Value

1. As a final step, confirm again and write out new or clarified core values you want to place your faith in for the future.

2. Spend some time in prayer committing your mind and heart to the core value the Lord and Scripture have led you to clearly establish. Ask for grace and faith to live in the core value you have now committed to.

The Process of Developing Core Values: In Relational Contexts of Life

The Process			
Identify Current Core Values →	Identify & Establish Biblical Core Values →	Repentance, Forgiveness, & Thanksgiving →	Commitment to Biblical CV
↓	↓	↓	↓
Often requires journey into the past	Seek biblical values through clear value mandates & implied in biblical illustrations	Col. 3:13/ Eph. 4:31, 32	Commit to the ongoing process refinement

We have chosen to identify and establish core values in six areas of human relationship and/or roles. Each individual experiences life in most of these six areas of life and relationship with others. We find it much easier to explore and establish one's core values within one of these six areas instead of one overall realm. It can certainly be done differently; however, we are approaching the process by examining our core values in these different "life" compartments.

- As self
- As a son or daughter
- As a husband or wife
- As a father or mother
- As a member of the Body of Christ in the community of believers
- As a member of the community at large outside the Body of Christ

The process begins by choosing one of these six areas to explore. We encourage starting with the area of self. The core values of self are the foundation from which so much of all other core values are established and impacted. Therefore, we strongly encourage beginning the process in this area of life and belief. It is the foundation for all our beliefs. However, as stated before, a person can begin with any one of the six areas. For our illustration of process, we will use self as our example.

Six Areas of Human Relationship and Roles to Consider:

As Self

Step One: **Identifying Current Core Values in the Different Role Areas of One's Life.**

Begin by praying and asking the Father, Son, and Holy Spirit to guide you through this process. We need His direction, knowledge, discernment, and wisdom to lead us through this entire process. This is essential and allows the Holy Spirit to have control of the process. Therefore, your pathway and experience may be different than what we are suggesting as the way to do this process.

After praying and asking the Holy Spirit to lead you through this process, continue by   considering several questions regarding this area of your life. As you consider each question, write down the first answers and thoughts that come to mind. (We suggest you begin a journal during this process).

Self: Who I am? What do I believe about my own worth and value? What do others say about my worth, value, and who I am? What does God say about who and what I am? (There may be many other questions you can use to help you explore this area of your life.)

Often you will begin to discover statements you are familiar with that can be identified as "self talk."

Your self talk reveals many of your core values regarding self.

- "I will not _____"
- "I will never _____"
- "I am a _____"
- "I can't _____"
- "I always _____"

Many of our self-talk statements reflect a value spoken or modeled by our parents or other significant family members. They often reflect a reaction to, or a duplication of what we experienced in our family system. These self-talk statements often reveal our core values that are our basic beliefs about this area of our lives. They expose what we truly believe about ourselves.

These self-talk statements and thoughts can also be connected to vows or promises we have made to ourselves after one or many experiences that created a certain self-belief. Many times, these beliefs are based upon a deception that is contrary to what God states is true about us. Thus, we have given permission or ground to certain deceptive beliefs that become powerfully unhealthy and affect many other areas of our self core values. Often these vows or promises are founded upon a lie, deception, and/or distorted biblical truth.

Again, before going on, ask the Holy Spirit to reveal your self-talk statements (core-value statements) and write them down. Ask the Holy Spirit to reveal any vows or promises you have made in the past. Self-talk statements like "I will never . . ." or "I will always . . ." can reveal vows we have established in our hearts and minds. This may take some time and this can be a long-term, ongoing process.

When a person purposely begins to explore and identify this area of self, it can be overwhelming. Or, some find it difficult to identify clear points about what they believe and/or know about themselves. Below, you will find some help to continue the process. To fully complete this process, it most often requires that we journey into our past. This can be difficult and it may take some time. Many, who have been serious about entering this journey, find that they stay in the process—one never fully finishes the process. Furthermore, some who have experienced severe abuse or trauma may require help from someone who is gifted and experienced in helping those in this situation.

Our Values and Beliefs Regarding Self Have Developed Primarily From:

Family System
- Significant moments and influence from our parents, grandparents, siblings, etc.
- Positive and negative

Religious/Early Church (or Non-Church) Experience
- Denominational distinctive
- Key pastoral/church leaders
- Personal experiences

Cultural Influence
- Peers
- Media
- Regional distinctive

Educational influence
Personality distinctive
Other?

Our Journey Into the Past

Questions to consider:

How do my self-talk statements connect to my family-system experience?

How did your family express who you were? (Usually established and remembered from particular moments and events.)

They may have been felt rather than spoken.

What are the significant events and experiences of your childhood and youth (ages birth-17)?

You may want to create a timeline of your life experiences.

Remember, it is not unusual for this to take some significant time. Often the Holy Spirit has a way of bringing up memories from time-to-time as one walks continually through the process. Trust the Spirit to do this as He wills.

What were some of the distinctive beliefs of your family?

For example: "We don't ask for help," or "We don't cry!"

What are some positive and negative experiences you had in the family you were raised in?

Did your religious system have any affect upon your idea of self?

How did the culture influence your concept of self?

- Peers
- Media
- Education
- Regional influences
- Other

What are other experiences, people, or things that have shaped your ideas about yourself?

Step Two: Identify Biblical Core Values

After beginning the process of identifying our current core values and beliefs about self, it is time to explore the Scriptures and identify what God says about who we are. The same questions can be used in this step. What does God say about our value and worth? What are the promises He has made to us that identify who we are?

Direct mandates and biblical illustrations regarding self in relationship with God

- Created in the Godhead's image (Gen.1:26)
- I am wonderfully made (Ps. 139:14)
- Heirs of God (tripartite promise: "I will be Your God, you will be My people, and I will dwell with you." Gen. 12-Rev. 21:3; Rom. 4:13; and 1 Pet. 1:3,4; Rom. 8:17)
- 1 Pet. 2:9 (Royal priesthood, holy nation)
- God loves us fully and has proven it (John 3:16)
- I am a new creation (2 Cor. 5:17)
- We are God's children and joint heirs with His Son (John 1:12, 1 John 4:1-6, Rom. 8:14,15)
- I am blessed (Deut. 28:1-6)
- I am a citizen of heaven (Phil. 3:20, Ps. 15)
- Nothing can separate us from God's love (Rom. 8:35-39)
- I am a friend of God (John 15:15)

What else does the Bible reveal to us about who we are in Christ?

Write any Scripture references, or write out the text in your journal. You may want to place past incorrect core values or beliefs next to the biblical truth that reveals the true value or belief you want to establish and begin to develop in your core.

Example:

"I can't do anything right"/"I can do all things through Christ who strengthens me." (Phil. 4:13)

Step Three: Repentance, Forgiveness, and Thanksgiving (if Needed)

Journeying into the past, often stirs up negative experiences, wounds, and mistakes but, also, positive, thankful feelings! As this happens, the following steps should be considered to help bring healing and freedom to rebuild healthy core values about yourself.

- Identify deceptions of belief (strongholds of wrong core values).
- 2 Cor. 10:3-6 Renounce them and commit to new belief!
- Identify duplication or reaction to our family, cultural, religious systems.
- Renounce wrong duplication or reaction and commit to new value.
- Repent: Release from past mistakes, vows, and revealed sin.
- Forgive: Release others from their mistakes that touched our lives. Col. 3:13 and Eph. 4:31-32.
- Express gratefulness and thankfulness (for freedom from whatever past experiences and deceptions have had their power in our lives).

Step Four: Making a Commitment to Healthy, Biblical, True Core Values

We have been clearly identifying many core values in one of the six areas (we have been focusing upon self) and evaluating them next to biblical values we have discovered and acknowledged as true. Now it is time to make clear, core-value statements that we will begin to believe and commit ourselves to for the future. Remember, this is often an ongoing process. However, we must identify and make a commitment to the core values we believe to be true and right

Make a list of the core values you believe are true and worthy of your commitment to believe and establish as who you are in Christ.

After making the list (knowing you will most likely add to the list in the future), offer a prayer of commitment to these values, and ask God to give you the grace and faith to allow them to be fully established in your life. You may also want to share them with your spouse or a trusted friend to help add accountability to your process.

Example:

I was created to be a son/daughter of my Creator God. I have a Father in heaven who protects and provides for me.

My value and worth come from the reality that God loves me fully because I am His son/daughter. I know that I am his son/daughter because I have surrendered myself to His love by acknowledging my need for salvation through the life, death, and resurrection of Jesus Christ.

I have a purpose and calling within the Kingdom of God and His plan for my life on this earth. I have been given the opportunity to be a "vessel of honor" that God can both pour into and out of in this life.

Final Core Value Statement and Belief Regarding Self:

I am a son of Father God, and my value comes through the reality of the Father's love, the Death and Resurrection of His Son Jesus, and the constant indwelling of the Holy Spirit in my life.

APPENDIX E

One way to engage in the Core Value process is to do it in a small group setting. Below are a few suggestions for the facilitator who is leading the group.

Suggestions for Small Group Leaders:

The purpose of each small group is to focus on one area of Core Value Development.
They will focus upon one area by:

1. Evaluating current core values.
2. Seeking God's Word for true, life-giving values.
3. Establishing specific core values to continue or establish in the one area of choice.
4. Committing to the process of establishing these values in everyday living.

The role of the small group leader is to:

1. Share personal process and journey in one area of life.
2. Facilitate discussion, exploration, and development that will help each person   begin (or continue) the process in their own lives.
3. Direct the group in looking together and identifying biblical and practical core values in the focused area.
4. Encourage each person to make a strong commitment toward implementing the values they have identified.
5. Follow-up with each person in the group throughout the next twelve months.

Suggestions and Tips for Small Group Leaders:

1. Record your own process and journey in the area you are focusing upon (this is a must).

2. Put it into a simple, written form that can be handed out and used as a starting place for discussion.

3. Use the exercise form(s) provided, or create a form that each person can use during their personal time to evaluate, develop, and process their core values.

4. Some of the small group time or personal time can be used to have participants find biblical examples that will help in establishing right core values.

5. The last session together should be used as a time for individuals to voluntarily share what they have discovered and determined during this time of focus (if this is too difficult for anyone, don't force them to share publicly).

6. Encourage a commitment component, and if possible, conclude with a time of prayer for each person either two-by-two or as the whole group.

This is a real life example of a couple creating core values as a part of establishing a plan and vision for the future in their ministry life.

Core Values in Our Relationships and Ministry

Spiritual Health

We believe that we are only effective through the strength, help, and direction of the Lord. If our intimacy with Him is not our first thought, we will not be useful to Him. We desire, in all we do, to be ambassadors for Christ. All that we do must be in Him, through Him, and with Him.

We don't want to do things in our own strength. We believe that the Lord speaks to us and wants to equip us for every good work. Therefore:

1. We commit to pursue love relationships with Jesus Christ as the most important aspect of our lives.
2. We commit to pursue His gifts and use them in His service.
3. We commit to walk in wisdom through Christ, that is *"pure, then peace-loving, considerate, submissive, full of mercy and good fruit, impartial and sincere"* (James 3:17, NIV).

Things for the next year.

1. We don't study the Word together. We will begin doing that this year.
2. I don't have accountability here. I have a friend far away I talk to every few weeks but desire someone here to connect deeply with. The men I did have accountability with have moved in the past six months. I need to reestablish community that way.

    3. My wife needs to know that I care for her walk with the Lord, that I am covering her, and that He is providing a covering for her.

Marriage

We are committed to our marriage as man and wife, but we are also best friends. We talk about everything and share everything. We need to guard our marriage against attacks. Our marriage is so much of what makes our ministry, our children, and our lives successful. The enemy wants to destroy our marriage and, with a domino effect, impact so many other things. We are committed to keeping our marriage strong. To make sure this happens, we will not allow outside influences to negatively impact our marriage. We will make it a priority in all our decisions.

    1. We will go out on a weekly date.
    2. If we have or see any problems, we will connect with others and nip those problems "in the bud" early. My wife can discuss issues of concern with others without my consent, and I can discuss issues of concern with others without her consent. "Others" would be people who we both recognize as having a voice in our lives.
    3. We view ourselves as accountable to these people and will welcome any input.

Children

Our children are more important than our work. Having stated that clearly, we believe we are called to work in another country, our children are called to work here with us, and we can be a healthy family, with healthy children, in fulfilling our calling. As we make decisions, about time commitments, or ministry direction, we will take our children into account first. Their spiritual, physical, emotional, and educational health will factor ahead of other considerations.

If we do not take care of our children first, we will have problems that will negatively impact our family and our work wherever we are and may even take us back to our homeland. After fifteen months in this country, we think our children are very healthy and have adjusted very well, and our family is "life giving." For that to continue, our children must know they are a priority.

Things for this next year:

A. Read to and teach the children to study the Word. We read the Word daily, and discuss it, but I need to be more intentional with my children in teaching them to study the Word.

B. We will continue to spend time working with youth. We believe that there is a huge need with the youth, and not only feel called to work with them, but we really want to and enjoy it. Seeing our children's friends be challenged and growing, and spending time with them is important for the health of our own children here in this place. Working with our children's friends is an important way for us to oversee our children's health.

C. Prayer – The community here is in constant transition. Friends come and go. Our children need good friendships.

Ministry

A. Our lives will have margin and quiet

A core value for our ministry and lives is that we will have margins. We have seen how busy we can get, and it doesn't do us or anybody else any good. We will have space in our lives to not always be at the point of exhaustion or having our schedules maxed out. When we see this happening, we will pull back, evaluate, and make the necessary adjustments, even if they are difficult because we are removing a good thing. We will not operate under the tyranny of the urgent.

B. Listening to God's Voice

There are so many voices in life that will try to tell you how to do things or plot life courses for you. As a core value, we commit to seeking God's direction for our ministry. We believe that we are to hear God's voice and then walk in what He says. We will seek council and direction from mature believers who know us and will confirm our direction or council us to pray about changing, but we believe we are to act on what the Lord is telling us and not be led by the opinions of others or what feels good.

C. Hospitality/Care

The Lord has given us a desire to care for others, and He also has given us gifts in this area. We function well together in taking care of others, encouraging others, and providing a safe place for people. We see this area as a way for us to help the work here in this country.

Financial Accountability

We commit to staying out of debt. There may be circumstances that arise that make this impossible, but to the extent that we have control, we will remain debt free. We will discuss our expenses and finances monthly with our leaders and will tell them when we have spent more than we have available.

We will keep our finances on a very short leash and not allow anything to get out of hand.

Reliance on God for Our Finances

We have seen the Lord provide for us for seven years. He has provided for us through moves, the ups and downs of life, major illness, and major transitions. We realize that He knows our needs better than we do. We will continue to rely on Him. A core value we have is that we are in His hands, and we will not fear or doubt if things get tight. We have seen him provide through extreme circumstances. We will never panic or manipulate our supporters because of fear or lack of faith. We believe in raising friends, not raising support. Therefore, all that we do will be about building relationships, not building a support base.

Hudson Taylor said, "God's work, done God's way, will not lack God's support." We believe this statement. If we ever do lack, we will pray but also seek council from those over us about our ministry and life direction concerning our work seeking their council about direction.

Language Study

We have not put as heavy of a priority on language over the past year as we should have. We will prioritize our schedules however we must to see that we grow in our language skills. I must make sure that my wife is freed from the home and children to be able to pursue language. This also includes language for the children. They will study our country's culture more intensely this year, as well.

10/8/17 - 1 Samuel 6:14

CV- OWE NO MAN NOTHING BUT
    LOVE. (ONE THING AT A TIME)

APPENDIX G

If you would like to schedule a retreat or seminar to explore and process this topic, we can be contacted at:

Rejoice Ministries International
4400 Pierce Dr.
Norfolk, NE 68701
Phone: 402-379-5224
Or at:
rejoiceministriesinternational.com